THE
POWER
OF
PASTA

THE POWER OF PASTA

»»➤ OF ◀«««

PASTA

A Celebrity Chef's Mission to Feed America's Hungry Children

INCLUDES 43 RECIPES FROM THE AWARD-WINNING ANAHEIM WHITE HOUSE RESTAURANT

BY BRUNO SERATO
WITH LORI HETHERINGTON

SelectBooks, Inc.

New York, New York

This edition published by SelectBooks, Inc.

For information address SelectBooks, Inc., New York, New York.

First Edition

ISBN 978-1-59079-435-7

Library of Congress Cataloging-in-Publication Data

Names: Serato, Bruno, author.
Title: The power of pasta : a celebrity chef's mission to feed America's hungry children : includes 40 recipes from the award-winning Anaheim White House Restaurant / by Bruno Serato with Lori Hetherington.
Description: First edition. | New York : SelectBooks, Inc., [2017] | Includes
bibliographical references.
Identifiers: LCCN 2017003324 | ISBN 9781590794357 (hardbound book : alk. paper)
Subjects: LCSH: Serato, Bruno. | Cooks--United States--Biography. | Anaheim White House Restaurant. | Caterina's Club. | Food relief--California--Orange County. | Cooking, Italian. | LCGFT: Cookbooks.
Classification: LCC TX649.S255 A3 2017 | DDC 641.5092 [B] --dc23 LC record available at https://lccn.loc.gov/2017003324

Jacket and design by Janice Benight

Manufactured in the United States of America
10 9 8 7 6 5 4 3 2 1

To Mamma Caterina, the inspiration behind the foundation
And to my father, Delio

Mamma Caterina surrounded by her loving family

CONTENTS

Foreword: A Hero Who Is Also a Friend ix

Introduction: It All Began with Love xiii

I. Home Is Where Your Heart Is 1

II. The American Dream 17

III. The Motel Kids 39

IV. Heroes...Big and Small 47

V. The Pastathon 67

VI. Life Is a Combination of Magic and Pasta 75

VII. The Hospitality Academy 85

VIII. Kind Words Are the Music of the World 91

IX. Italy–The Land of Love and Generosity 97

X. Always Listen to Your Mamma 113

XI. New Beginnings 121

RECIPES 147

Appetizers/Small Plates 149

Entrees 171

Desserts 225

Acknowledgments 239

Recipe Index 243

Index 245

About the Author 253

Awards Received 255

FOREWORD:
A HERO WHO IS ALSO A FRIEND

In San Bonifacio, Italy, not far from where I was born and live with my family, a true modern-day hero spent his youth: Bruno Serato.

I use the term "true modern-day hero," but what does it really mean? And who are these heroes of our times?

Actually, it is easier to look for and find them than one might think. Look around, pay close attention, and learn from people who have reawakened their sense of conscience and brought forward the innate compassion that is part of us all. It requires training and practice every day, so that the "hero" within us learns to step forward, with a gesture as simple as an offering.

Seven days a week, Bruno prepares more than 1,800 pasta dinners for hungry children. He is not only satisfying their need for food but is also filling and nourishing their hearts with hope and great love. Bruno is an example of a modern-day hero, and he offers us this model of behavior, renewing what it means to be a human being. In a world where it sometimes feels as if passing values are imposed on us, the altruism of simplicity may exist, and resist, within a famous restaurant, or perhaps just outside our door.

Bruno is promoting heroism and is showing us how to do it. He has, up to now, served more than *one million* plates of pasta to children in need. Those children have a right to not be hungry and, by taking action and "doing," Bruno's commitment takes on a heroic aspect. When a child has a wholesome plate of pasta in his or her stomach, he or she can play, study, and participate in life.

Thanks to Bruno, and thanks to all the modern heroes, we can, together, one day achieve something truly important. We should never look for excuses for not taking action: Only action can transform a utopia into a dream, and a dream into a reality.

From the depths of my heart, thank you, Bruno, for all that you do! You have committed yourself to helping those who are less fortunate get ahead through your wonderful association. With equal parts of passion and true dedication you also "feed" us all every day, acting as a guide and example for the heroes of tomorrow.

Welcome, Bruno, to our Heroes Company. It is an honor to have you on our team!

With deep friendship and sincere admiration,

ROBERTO BAGGIO
World Soccer Player of the Year, 1993

(left) Bruno at headquarters of Barilla,
the largest pasta factory in the world
in Parma, Italy

INTRODUCTION:
IT ALL BEGAN WITH LOVE

"Not all of us can do great things.
But we can do small things with great love."

–MOTHER TERESA

"Excuse me, Bruno. Do you remember me?"

I studied the friendly features of the young man as I prepared to serve pasta at the Boys and Girls Club of Anaheim in California. His dark eyes were filled with hope.

The room was buzzing with excited, mostly elementary school-aged children who could hardly sit still. It was five o'clock in the afternoon, and we were about to dish up the steaming pasta my assistants and I had brought from the restaurant.

I speak to a lot of people during an average week and he'd caught me by surprise. There was something familiar about his face but I couldn't place it.

"I'm sorry, no," I replied.

He extended his hand and his face brightened. "It's me, Billy," he said. "I was one of the first kids you served."

That day—April 18, 2005—came rushing back to me, and the memory of how one boy changed my life and filled my heart to overflowing.

"Oh my God!" My hands covered my mouth in shocked surprise. "It's great to see you, Billy. How are you?"

I knew the answer just by looking at him. Gone were the dirty clothes and the worn shoes. Here was a handsome young man, ready to take his place in the adult world. His hair was neat, his shirt was tucked in, and he stood up straight and tall. He told me with pride that he'd graduated from high school and was working full time for the Boys and Girls Club. He hugged me and thanked me for making a difference in his life, then went back to work helping the younger kids. Tears stung my eyes. If only my mom could have been there.

The first time I saw Billy ten years ago, he was eating a small bag of potato chips. The kind you buy in a vending machine. Not such an odd thing for a seven-year-old but, as I discovered, that was probably his dinner. His entire dinner.

On that day my mother, Caterina Lunardi, and I were at the Boys and Girls Club because I was on the local board of directors, and Disneyland, located less than three miles away, was going to present the club with an important donation.

Mamma was visiting from Italy for the winter, as she usually did in those years despite her Parkinson's disease, to stay with me and my sister, Stella. I loved when she came because finally *I* was the one taking care of *her*.

Whenever someone mentioned kids, Mamma's face would light up, so I knew that she'd enjoy this event. An Italian mother of seven, and grandmother of twenty, Mamma adored children's shining eyes, warm embraces, and laughter. Italian mammas love *bambini*.

Mike Baker, the Executive Director of the Boys and Girls Club at the time, gave Mamma a tour and told her about their programs and, although I was already well acquainted with the club's good work, I remained close by her side. I knew her Parkinson's was giving her trouble that day, even if she never complained. The after-school kids were excited when visitors came and they were thrilled to see us. A group of girls insisted on showing Mamma how fast they could skip Dutch double rope. A boy ran up to me and tugged on my sleeve.

"Watch this!" he said snapping his wrist, a yo-yo humming as it circled through the air.

The chorus of playground voices—dozens of children playing in safe surroundings—brought smiles to our faces. Mike drew our attention to Billy, who was standing nearby.

"Unfortunately, that's probably all he'll eat between now and the time he goes to bed. He could be a motel kid. We've got lots of them here," Mike said.

"What's a motel kid?" I asked. I thought a motel was a cheaper option than a hotel, and you stayed in one because you were on vacation.

"Some of the boys and girls live in motels because their parents can't afford the rent for an apartment. Whole families in tiny motel rooms, dingy places that are often infested with bugs. Even if their moms want to make them dinner, they don't have a kitchen to cook in."

Children going to bed with empty stomachs? Living in the darkest environment imaginable, a place known for prostitution, gangs, drugs, and pedophiles? And on top of all that, they were going hungry? I remember I shook my head and felt a stone drop into the pit of my stomach. I could hardly believe this was happening in my own backyard, right here in the United States of America. I had no idea there were children living in my neighborhood who were starving. How could they look up at the moon and stars and dream their dreams if they were hungry? My heart broke.

Mamma set a trembling hand on my arm. *"Cosa c'è, Bruno?"* she asked, worried that I'd suddenly fallen ill.

I translated what Mike had said. I knew, from my own upbringing, that Mamma couldn't stand to see children deprived of the warmth and nourishment of good, wholesome food. A part of me expected her to cry out in horror, but I should have known better. If anyone knew how to deal with a bunch of hungry kids, it was my mom. Even though we'd been poor, there was always a place at our table for anyone who needed to eat.

"Bruno," she said, looking up into my eyes, "Why don't you make some pasta for these kids?"

Pasta. That was something I could do. Besides, I could never say no to Mamma. "We'll be right back," I told Mike.

Mamma and I hurried to the car and drove the short distance back to my restaurant, Anaheim White House, where preparations were underway for that night's dinner service. My chefs were busily chopping vegetables, slicing top-grade beef, perfecting the dishes we'd serve in a few hours; the dining room staff was arranging fresh flowers for the tables and setting out the crystal. Mamma and I went straight to the kitchen and tied on aprons. We filled a big pot with water, put it on to boil, and whipped up some fresh tomato sauce.

Mamma Caterina and Chef Bruno in the kitchen at Anaheim White House

About an hour later, we loaded spaghetti into the car and drove back. More than fifty children, including Billy, were still at the club when we arrived carrying the heavy, restaurant-sized pot, still hot from the stove. We set it down on a table. When Mamma took off the aluminum foil, the comforting aroma of that humble but satisfying meal I had eaten every single day when I was growing up hit me with the full force of my mother's love and protection. It gave me such joy to share it with those kids, and seeing the same happiness in my Mamma made it all the better. Before long, the boys and girls had devoured every last bite.

"Thank you, Bruno!" they called out one at a time as they lined up for the van that would take them back to the motel, or wherever they'd sleep that night.

"That was great," said Mike, shaking my hand. "Thanks."

Later that evening, after the restaurant had closed, I sat down with Mamma to have a late-night espresso. There, in my tiny office, I finally voiced what had been bothering me since we'd left the Boys and Girls Club with the empty pot.

"Those kids may not go to bed hungry tonight," I told her, "but they will tomorrow."

Mamma's blue eyes sparkled and her face softened into the smile I'd known all my life. A knowing, mother's smile. "Then feed them again tomorrow," she told me. "No child should go to bed hungry."

Italy and food: One does not—cannot—exist without the other. We Italians love our food, and we take eating very seriously. Like many Italian couples, my parent's love story began because of food. For them, it was a watermelon. It was oval and perfectly ripe, its mottled rind the color of the Italian country-side. The same colors as the landscape that flew past the window of the train on which the watermelon traveled. This particular train was journeying along its usual route between Vicenza and Villanova, Italy, in the year 1944. Villa-nova is near Soave, the center of the production zone for the dry, fruity white wine of the same name that is famous all over the world. A land of vineyards and crenellated castles. Two of the train's many passengers were my mamma and her best friend, Raffaella—who would later become her sister by marriage when she married my mother's brother—and they were discussing the issue of the watermelon. As appetizing as the giant fruit looked and smelled, it simply could not be eaten because they were without a knife.

It was summer, and it was hot and humid. Mamma and Raffaella had found the big, smooth, ripe watermelon in a field, and they were taking it home. The smell emanating from it seemed to grow stronger and stronger as the heat in the train compartment rose. The girls were proud of their treasure and couldn't wait to share it with the rest of their families. They giggled and squirmed as they dreamed of how it would quench their thirst, how they could tell it was sweet from the sound it made when they knocked on it with their knuckles, and how excited everyone at home would be when they arrived with the delicious fruit.

What these two young women did not realize was that another passenger, seated on the bench directly across from them, was listening in on their conversation and was just dying to talk to the beautiful woman with long, dark hair: Mamma. The passenger's name was Delio, a handsome young man who looked just like the soon-to-be-famous actor, James Dean. Noting that he could be of assistance, Delio offered up the knife he had been using to peel an apple as a way to start a conversation. That way they could taste the watermelon to make sure it really was sweet. And that's when he asked her name.

"Caterina," Mamma replied. Her hands shook as she reached for the knife. The stranger was the most attractive man she had ever seen.

Why had she not noticed him before?

Her stomach flipped with nervous excitement and, against her will, sparks popped, sizzled, and ignited. After all, she was engaged to a man from the south of Italy, and their families were currently in the process of arranging their Catholic wedding. The next month was full of events in preparation for the ceremony, including a big engagement party. She had no business feeling charmed by such a stunning man. However, the least she could do, she told herself, was

Mamma Caterina at 20 years old

carve out a slice of watermelon for him. It wouldn't hurt to offer him a slice of the fruit as a way to say *grazie*, would it?

They met again unexpectedly a month later on the same train. Without the watermelon as a subject of conversation, they spoke about themselves and everything else under the Italian sun, while Raffaella sat nearby as unofficial chaperone.

Caterina told Delio about how at the age of nine she had tended sheep and cows in a hamlet called Gallio in the northern Italian mountains where she lived with her grandparents, parents, and siblings. It was a place of sweet green pastures, where the music of cowbells bigger than your hand and smaller, fist-sized ones on the sheep rang through the air as the little herd grazed to the song of mountain thrushes. She loved the animals and knew them all by the names she gave them, her favorites being Derna, Fortuna, and Bianca.

When Delio told Caterina he was the oldest of five siblings and that his father had died nine years before and his mother not long afterwards at the age of thirty-eight, Caterina tried to imagine how a young man could live with such heartache. As he told it, he'd become the man of the house and had taken his brothers and sisters under his wing. He peddled anything he could find in order to keep them from starving.

As the train arrived at the station, and they prepared to go their separate ways, Delio knew he had to do something to keep Caterina from walking out of his life. He watched the two young women thread their way along with the other passengers as they looped back around the other side of a chain-link fence to head into the station.

"Do I at least get a kiss?" he called out.

Caterina didn't say anything, but she stopped while the other passengers flooded past her in their hurry to get somewhere else. Then she stepped closer, and that was when my mother and father kissed for the first time, their lips coming together between the links in the fence.

After that kiss, Mamma knew she had to break off her engagement. On April 9, 1945, three weeks before Mussolini was arrested and executed, my parents got married. It must have been love at first sight. Raffaella and Attilio, Mamma's only brother, decided to get married on the same day, and there was one big celebration in the town. The reception was at the farmhouse called La Fabrica, not far from the Alpone river, close to my grandparent's home. As is typical for weddings in Italy, a huge (yet affordable) banquet was served for the guests: The menu included lamb, polenta, and pasta—lots of pasta. Years later, I would serve that same pasta recipe to the people I care about and love.

It seemed that maybe the future *was* getting brighter.

One of the fondest memories from my childhood is of a frigid, snowy day when my old, worn shoes weren't sturdy enough to get me to school. I was eight years old and probably the fifth or sixth boy to wear those shoes. They'd been handed down to our family from our neighbors across the street, like most of the things we wore. Even though the clothes were sometimes stained or already threadbare when they got to us, we thought they were exciting and new. Corrado, my older brother, always had first pick. If something was too small for him, I could claim it, and when he outgrew the pants, jacket, or shoes, they eventually became mine.

These particular shoes were once, I believe, brown leather but had become so scuffed and hard that they had become a non-color. Not brown, not black. Just shoes. The type of lace-up, high-top shoes that children wore in Europe to go to school, to play, to do chores, and sometimes wore to bed if the night was particularly cold. The heavy twine that threaded through the eyelets had been knotted more than once and the soles had come away from the uppers where my growing feet struggled to break free, the leather thin from a million adventures with friends and battles with siblings. On the right, at the tip. On the left, over my little toe, with my sock about to break through the cardboard-like sole.

Normally it took me thirty minutes to walk from our two-room house in the tiny village of Chaillevois to the nearest schoolhouse. A dusty road when the weather was dry and a string of puddles, like pearls on a necklace, when it rained. My feet usually hardly took notice. But when the weather turned cold, I became painfully aware of each step through the snow.

My parents had moved to the Picardy region of northern France—a mostly flat, agricultural land that in one corner touches the border with Belgium—before I was born. In the early 1950s life had yet to improve in Italy after the war. Fascism, World War II and its aftermath, and years of struggling to recover all combined to create a dismal situation throughout Italy, including the northern region of Veneto where my parents originated. Many men, as well as entire families, emigrated northward toward France and Belgium, where there were plenty of resources but a shortage of able-bodied workers. In 1951 my parents made the biggest decision of their lives: They packed up and left their homeland. They went to pick vegetables on the farms in the north; the pay was better than nothing and at least there would be food.

By the time I arrived at school in those hand-me-down shoes on that freezing day in winter, my feet were blistered and numb, and I still had to trudge home when school ended. I didn't say anything to Mamma when I walked in the door. I knew how busy she was, taking care of me and my six siblings, cooking our meals, cleaning the house, washing our clothes in the fountain at the village square, bent over for long hours every day picking beets and potatoes on Monsieur Simphal's farm, and putting up with my hot-tempered father. We lived in a tiny house with a kitchen, one bedroom, and no running water, and despite the hard labor Mamma endured and the small wages my dad brought home from driving a truck whenever he got the chance, we were better off than we would have been living in Italy.

When I woke up the following morning, snow covered the ground and was still falling. Thought of the long walk to school obliterated any notice of its beauty.

Mamma hugged me and said, "Why don't you stay home with me today, Bruno?" She must have read my mind. A smile drove away my stoic expression.

It was a rare treat to be alone with Mamma, and I followed her around all day like a little duckling. I watched her effortlessly knead together flour and water to make fresh pasta for lunch and helped her stir the tomato sauce. She let me taste it from a wooden spoon, the delicate flavors of herbs and summer tomatoes canned in jars on a sunny day warming even my cold feet. Except for holidays, we always ate the same meals: pasta with tomato sauce for lunch and warm milk with a splash of coffee and leftover bread for supper. We were miserably poor, but on Sundays we were lucky. Mamma would wake up extra early to make bread, fresh gnocchi, and a roast duck or chicken. The simple food Mamma cooked for us was always made with such love that we hardly noticed our economic circumstances.

A young Bruno with his sister Flavia circa 1960

Bruno at nine years old with his younger brother Silvano

Despite her busy daily routine, when one of Mamma's best friends and a fellow immigrant from next-door, Maria Guarda, dropped by midmorning— after my brothers and sisters had gone to school and Papa had left for work— Mamma stopped everything to make a fresh pot of coffee.

"How about one of your famous apple tarts, Delia?" Maria asked, using my mother's nickname. In no time, Mamma mixed up a few of the ingredients she'd been saving for a special occasion and slid three small apple tarts into the oven. Our home was little more than a shack, but whenever someone came for a visit, Mamma treated them like royalty. I watched and learned.

The education I received on that one day at home was surely far more valuable than any lesson the teacher had planned. Hospitality is a learned skill and my teacher was the best.

Decades later and a continent away, I put into practice the lessons I'd learned from watching Mamma. As a way to honor her, I began hosting annual luncheons at my restaurant for a group of women from the area. I called the events Caterina's Club and, with a desire to make a contribution to my community, I donated the proceeds from the events to help support services for local children through the Boys and Girls Club of Anaheim. The first of these ladies' luncheons took place in 2003. Just two years later, Mamma encouraged me to make pasta for the kids at the club, which transitioned into our wider-reaching Feeding the Kids in America program, and we simply kept the name that was already in place. Our aim was to not only fill the stomachs of the most vulnerable children but also to fill their hearts and minds as well. Although most of the children served by Caterina's Club have access to government-subsidized school breakfasts and lunches, nutritious meals outside school hours are essential too if we want our children to grow up healthy.

Orange County is well known for its beauty and the lavish lifestyles of some of the people who live there. But only some. Nearly 15 percent of Orange County residents struggle on a daily basis to have their food needs met, and many of those living in food-insecure households are children—and often food insecurity goes hand in hand with homelessness. While Orange County has a high rate of food insecurity, this problem is widespread throughout the United States—more so than many people realize. We strive to remedy this problem.

I've always enjoyed good food and the atmosphere created when people sit down around a table together. The breaking of the bread embodies the most ancient of rituals that unite people, nourishing body and spirit, and making it possible to overcome life's difficulties so that joy can burst forth.

Just as Mamma taught me, guests are special. No matter who they are or what's brought them to your doorstep, they deserve to be treated with love and attention.

When I plan the menu for a special Caterina's Club event at the restaurant, I try to think of what my guests will appreciate most, and one course of the meal is always pasta! When my guests are children, I usually serve at least two different types of pasta because some of them love to suck the strands of spaghetti—which means "little strings" in Italian—into their mouths, and some find it difficult to manage. When I see children eating pasta made under my careful supervision, with ingredients I've chosen especially for their young bodies, I feel like a proud, loving parent watching his children grow. For the rest of the menu, I consider what's in season, what I know they'll eat, and what will be attractive on the plate.

More than just serving them dinner, we encourage them to participate by setting the tables, serving one another, and stewarding conversation. Sharing the table provides the children with an opportunity to experience camaraderie and family values that promote confidence in their day-to-day lives. Table settings and etiquette are important, too. Many of the children have never been in a restaurant before, let alone a fine-dining establishment. It is important to me that the children get to experience this to give them hope that life in not just a classroom, a motel room, or an after-school club. So I invite them all to dine at my restaurant every year to experience a Thanksgiving feast. We arrange both long and round tables in the same dining rooms we use for our most exclusive parties, and when the children walk into the room their eyes get big, trying to take it all in. Children are my favorite customers.

Our first Caterina's Club Thanksgiving dinner, for 450 children, was in 2007. *Mamma mia*, what fun! I had ten tons of snow blown in on the front lawn of the restaurant and let the kids play in it after they'd eaten. Most of them had never before seen snow. They squealed with delight and gathered it up to make snowballs with their bare hands, the skin on their palms quickly turning pink. To my surprise, their favorite target was Chef Bruno! There wasn't a sad face in the bunch. After having suffered my own troubles with snow, I was thrilled to share the beauty and fun of one of nature's wonders.

Through the generosity of local media outlets, including radio and television stations and other donors, we've been able to increase the number of diners at our annual feast for children and their families. We have countless

Chef Bruno and the kids from the Boys and Girls Club having spaghetti (photo by Tony Zuppardo)

Chef Bruno enjoying a silly moment with the kids (photo by Tony Zuppardo)

turkeys and tons of food, in addition to the tons of snow! We also always have lots of volunteers, including celebrities like Paul Sorvino and his Academy Award-winning daughter, Mira. Whenever I can, I like to include sports or entertainment celebrities in our Caterina's Club events. I believe it makes the children feel special, and they see that fame and success are attainable. Spending the day with happy children eating good food touches every volunteer's heart. It's satisfying and joyful work that makes a true difference for the kids and everyone involved.

I didn't always own a restaurant or have the resources to help kids in need. In fact, I was one of those kids myself in some ways, and I think that's why I felt so compelled to feed them.

I

HOME IS
WHERE YOUR HEART IS

"When you give a dinner or a banquet, do not invite your friends
or your brothers or your kinsmen or rich neighbors, lest they
also invite you in return, and you be repaid. But when you give
a feast, invite the poor, the maimed, the lame, the blind,
and you will be blessed, because they cannot repay you."

—LUKE 14:12-14

If you've ever visited Italy or seen pictures in a travel brochure, you probably noticed the beautiful architecture, the open-air markets full of colorful
fruits and vegetables, the carefully arranged shop windows, and the elegantly
dressed people sipping espresso. But those are relatively recent truths.

After the war, in the countryside around Verona in the north of Italy, the
roads were poorly paved, or not at all, and muddy or dusty depending on the
season; the few animals that had not been eaten by soldiers or hungry families
were skinny and produced poorly. There wasn't much of anything, especially if
you were like my parents and didn't have money. But there was always polenta
or pasta, and families found joy in sitting down together, even while painfully
aware that around hundreds of thousands of tables throughout the country
sat empty chairs that no longer held a husband or a son.

It wasn't the war or a lack of food that took my parent's firstborn son.
Instead, he tumbled from my mother's arms when he was six months old.

The young Serato family—my father, mother, and the first baby, Corrado— were crowded in the back of a truck together with other laborers on their way home after a long day's work. The mood was cheerful and merry—they'd harvested a good quantity of vegetables that day, my parents were in love, and they had a beautiful baby boy. The truck bounced along the pot-holed track as some of its passengers laughed over a joke, while others fell asleep, their limbs weary, the constant jostling like the rocking of a cradle. Several women huddled in a corner to gossip. It had rained in the early morning, and the clouds in the sky suggested it might rain again soon. In the gloom of the northern Italian dusk, the driver did his best to transport them all home as soon as possible. He was hungry and knew his wife was waiting with something warm for supper. Perhaps a pot of minestrone or polenta with some melted cheese.

Mamma sat in the back of the truck with Corrado nestled comfortably. He was drowsy, and she was happy that he'd settled into an easy routine that allowed her to work in the fields. He was a good baby—sleeping, eating, and rarely fussing.

Unexpectedly, the truck skidded down a riverbank after missing a turn and bumped over an exposed rock, and that's when the baby flew from Mamma's arms. Even before the vehicle had completely stopped, the men jumped over the side board and scrambled to retrieve the baby lying in a puddle, to return him thoroughly soaked to his desperate mother. She frantically checked to make sure he wasn't hurt, cooed and rocked him so he'd know he was safe, and thanked God for returning her little son to her.

Corrado caught pneumonia and died within the week.

For anyone who's ever lost a child, it is a wound that never completely heals. I still get a lump in my throat when I think of how my mother's heart, despite having suffered such a painful twist of fate, was more unselfish than any I've ever known.

There's something special about mothers. Whenever Mamma held a child in her arms, it was as if that child came from her own womb, even late in her life when her illness had taken away her ability to speak and full control of her muscles. She would rock the baby or bounce the toddler on her knee, love radiating from every inch of her own tiny body.

My parents went on to have other children. Before they left Italy in 1951, they had a daughter—my sister Stella—and then a son, who they named after their firstborn. My other siblings and I were born in France; I was born in the city of Laon.

Mamma had learned about generosity from her father, Giovanni Lunardi, a shepherd in a little village called Villanova in a mountainous area of green pastures, fruit trees, and grape vines. In fact, generosity and a concern for others is learned in childhood. The Lunardis were poor and Mamma and her entire family worked hard to survive, but because they were shepherds they always had something to eat. Simple food, like polenta and pasta, cheese, milk, and other bounties of the land. When people came to beg her father for food, he never refused anyone, even though they couldn't pay. They shared what they could with neighbors in need. In our home, it was always the same.

Our family life revolved around my parents' work, our school, and chores. Even if I slept poorly because my four brothers and I shared a bed (Freddy, the youngest, wiggled in his sleep or cried in the night), I knew that Mamma would always be there to help resolve our differences and set a warm plate of pasta with tomato sauce on the table for lunch, together with her unending love. Her presence was unwavering, even though the white potatoes and red beets she had to pick every day exhausted her. Her happiness was replenished by the sight of her children.

Like many Italian families, emigration has always been a part of our history. My great-grandfather on my mother's side emigrated to New York toward the end of the nineteenth century and returned home with enough money to buy a flock of sheep; some of Nonno's flock were direct descendants. Thanks to his success in overcoming hardship in the New World, the Lunardis never starved. We have had aunts, uncles, and cousins spread across the globe in Australia, the

United States, and all throughout Europe. When it was my parents' turn, they did what was necessary for their family, repeating essentially the same story.

When I was nine years old, my parents followed the flow of work opportunities to another town a short distance away. We said good-bye to our friends in Vivaise and packed up our few possessions. Life in Vivaise picking vegetables was hard, but the close-knit community of immigrant families helped brighten our days. No matter your language of origin, religion, or the traditional food cooked in your kitchen, the experience of living in a country that is not yours varies little in space or in time.

I think of all the people who, over the decades and centuries, including our present day, have left their beloved homes to seek something better, safer, or more promising in an unknown land; they deserve great respect. I recognize in them my parents and my great-grandfather, whom I never knew, and the others who've crossed the oceans. I'm connected to them all.

It seemed like we were moving halfway across the world. Mamma had been offered a chance to tend thousands of chickens in exchange for rent. A couple of years later, when Mamma and my oldest brother were hired to care for a herd of cows, the owner of the farm let us live in what seemed like a villa, but I realize now that it was just an old farmhouse. There were more bedrooms than we'd ever seen in one house and surely didn't need them all. First Mamma had tended chickens and we had a small house, and then she took care of cows and we had a big house. For years I thought the size of the animals you cared for determined how big your house was.

When we lived in France, sometimes traveling peddlers stopped by to sell their wares. Most people didn't have transportation beyond their own two feet, and outside of larger towns shops were rare. I remember one particular peddler. He was a small man compared to my father, and the folded carpets piled high on his shoulders hid half of his body. He was from Morocco and spoke French with a strong accent, but we were used to people with accents. Our village was full of immigrants from countries like Poland, Portugal, Ukraine, Slovakia, Spain, and Italy. Like us, they were people who worked hard in a land that was not theirs because the war had devastated their own. When my father told the peddler he couldn't afford to buy a carpet, the seller's face fell. No telling how many times he'd been refused that day.

Mamma was in the kitchen, rolling out the pasta dough and cutting it into strips to make fettuccine. "Cara," she said to my sister, using her favorite term of endearment, "set another place at the table."

My father helped the man set down his goods and held the door open for him. He was surprised. Not many people had invited him to sit at their family table before, but this was what my family was all about. *Viva la pasta!*

To this day, a whiff of tomato sauce is enough to make my mouth water and a warm feeling fill my belly. I see in my mind's eye Mamma's nimble, flour-covered hands and her sweet face peeking through the kitchen window, watching for us as we made our way home for lunch so she'd know when to put the pasta into the pot. Her favorite part of every day, until her last at the age of 90, was when we showed up for lunch. Sharing food and the good feelings of moments together is what drives me; it's what my mother taught me. In one simple dish—pasta—you've got it all: comfort, love, warmth, home. I can't live without it.

One day at the Boys and Girls Club I noticed a boy in a red t-shirt. His knee bounced under the table where he was sitting; his fingers fidgeted near his mouth. From the moment I'd walked into the dining room, his eyes were glued to the professional food service pan I carried. It was heavy, and when I set it down in the serving area it made a loud *thunk*.

The prep team had already completed their job: Everything was set up and ready—plastic plates and forks lined up neatly, small cartons of milk stacked for distribution—all we needed to do was dish up the pasta.

"Who's ready for pastaaaa?!" I called out.

The room filled with the voices of a hundred excited children, cheering and jumping up and down as if their favorite sports team had just won the most important game of the season. All their attention was on the bounty they were about to receive; they were hungry and could hardly wait to share the pleasure of their first forkful with each other.

I held out a plate piled high with spaghetti to the boy in the red t-shirt. He beamed. His front two teeth were missing, and his smile stretched from ear to ear. He reached out, and for a split second the plate held between us was like a bridge between his heart and mine. The strands of pasta were not only calories and vitamins to provide physiological nourishment but also love that boosts and sustains. The same meal I grew up on led me as an adult to stand there, in that room full of noisy, joyful, hungry children, sharing Mamma's love with each and every one of them.

Pasta nurtures the body and makes for unforgettable moments.

One of the kids happily eating pasta with Mamma Caterina's sauce   (photo by Tony Zuppardo)

My memories of those years in France include some of the most delicious food I've ever tasted. When we were lucky, our Ukrainian friends invited us to share a Sunday meal. Jeannine was a marvelous cook, and her husband, who everyone called "The Russian," was one of my three (yes, three!) godfathers. My entire family remembers them with great love, as we do so many of the people we met who were, like my parents, determined to make a better life for themselves and their families. Everyone shared in the joy when a baby was born, lent a hand when someone was ill, and mourned with a heavy heart when sad news arrived from home.

The community gathered round my parents when I was six months old. As the story goes, I woke up early in the morning, crying frantically. Mamma tried to comfort me, but I could not take her milk without vomiting and convulsing. Papa alerted the neighbors who took my brother and sisters to their home, and my parents rushed me to the nearest hospital. When the doctor finished examining me, he delivered awful news. My intestines were tangled, he said, and I probably would not survive—perhaps not even through the night. My parents were devastated. How could they endure the pain of losing another child? The doctor insisted they go home and call back in the morning. Parents were not allowed to remain by the bedside during the night.

Mamma prayed to Saint Anthony of Padua all through the dark hours. If he saved my life, she vowed, she would dress me as a monk for the next six months. I would be a living votive medal.

Shortly after sunrise, the baker came knocking on my parent's front door. He was the only person in the village who had a telephone, and the hospital had called. Mamma and Papa hurried back to the hospital on my father's motorcycle, fearful that I had died. When they arrived, a nurse led them into the darkened room where they'd left me the night before. Mamma broke into tears when she saw I had survived the night and was sleeping soundly. The doctor had no explanation for my recovery.

When my parents took me home, everyone rejoiced in what seemed like a miracle, and Mamma set to sewing up a tiny monk's habit, which I wore—as promised—for the next six months. When it was time for my christening, three men fought over the privilege to be my godfather. One of them Italian, one French, and the third "The Russian."

We moved several times during our years in France. Each new home wasn't far if you counted the actual miles as the bird flies, but leaving our friends behind tore at our hearts. And yet, certain things never changed. Thirty years later, when Mamma went back to Vivaise to visit for the first time after three decades, a woman recognized her at the market. The woman was so happy she rushed to the market office and asked to use the microphone.

"Attention, s'il vous plaît! Madame Serato est revenue!"

The love was still there. Mamma had a way of leaving her mark wherever she went.

In the summer of 1967, when I was eleven years old, Papa drove us all to Italy to visit Mamma's family. There were grandparents, aunts, uncles, and cousins, most of whom I'd only met in my parents' stories. We piled into my father's little blue Fiat for the 650-mile trip, the Serato family hardly able to wait another minute to visit our people.

A long, crusty baguette cut into nine pieces—and filled with as much cheap, finely sliced ham as Mamma could buy—was in a bag at her feet. I elbowed and squirmed in the backseat with my brothers and sisters and finally, once we were all settled, Papa let out the brake. We drove through France, Germany, Switzerland, and over the Alps, terrified as our little car rounded the curves, sheer cliffs plunging just inches from the edge of the asphalt. It was a relief to finally stop in a high mountain pasture, with our feet on solid ground. We crowded onto a plaid blanket surrounded by alpine wildflowers to eat our one sliver of sustenance during the fifteen-hour trip. We felt light as the breeze in the sunshine and fresh air, but family was waiting.

The hours stretched out and the space in the backseat seemed to shrink. If we had to stay in the car another minute, we were sure we'd explode. But then Papa started honking the horn: There were only two miles left before Villanova. He wanted to let everyone know we'd come home. When we reached the end of the road, there was a little old lady dressed in black. It was Nonna, and she'd been standing there all day long with her heart full of love, waiting for her daughter to return home with all of her *bambini*.

I was so happy to see my grandmother again. I loved her very much, and it had been years since she'd come to help lift some of the burden of four small children from my mother's shoulders. When Nonna came to stay with us in France, she showered us with grandmotherly love and her delicious stewed rabbit, while Mamma spent all day picking vegetables.

Nonno Giovanni was out with the flock when we arrived in Villanova. Late in the afternoon we heard the distant tinkling of sheep bells, and our cousins told us it was Nonno coming home with his herd of sheep.

My grandfather Nonno Giovanni with his flock

"Nonno! Nonno! Nonno!" we shouted as we jumped up and down, our hand-me-down shoes stamping in the dirt.

One of my fondest memories of Nonno is of him doing his hat trick. We were in awe; he was as good as a real magician! At bedtime, all of us kids would sit around him to listen to his stories, the same ones I share with my nieces and nephews today.

Mamma hadn't seen her family for nine years, and their tearful reunion was contagious, especially when she and her younger sister reunited; they shared a special bond right up until the end. The love that held them together was so strong you could feel it in the air; it had density and flavor. This is the same type of love that fuels me when I return to Italy today. Family is everything for Italians—protection, support, survival—wrapped up like a roast, the butcher's twine made of a shared history that stretches over generations to hold it tight. Sometimes people in a family don't agree and shout at each other, but that doesn't take away the love.

Mamma Caterina with her parents, Giovanni and Rosina, circa 1978

"When I grow up, I want to be a teacher."

"When I grow up, I want to be a marine."

"When I grow up, I want to be an artist."

"When I grow up, I want to be a doctor."

"When I grow up, I want to be a chef."

These are the words of children who can see a future.

When children are plagued by an empty stomach, and home is a place of fear and unhealthy conditions, how can they dream about tomorrow? If basic needs like hunger and a sense of security are absent, a person of any age can't imagine that something beyond today might exist.

When I was a boy, I dreamed of being a steward on an airplane. Air travel at that time was glamorous, exotic, and exciting, and I wanted to be a part of that world. Another dream I had for a short time was to become a monk. I knew a man in our village who had taken vows, and I wanted to be like him—simple, peaceful, caring. (Looking back, could my experience as a baby have had anything to do with my early desire for an ascetic life?)

I may no longer be a child who dreams of his future, but I still dream.

Someday I would like to cook pasta for my boss, the one who I'd better listen to because he has the power to fire me anytime he wants: God. I hope He lets me take the burden for a day and that I can serve Him. I hope He likes my pasta!

Faith is an important part of my life. Without faith, a person has nothing to grab onto when they're in need. The way I see it, faith is food for the soul and everyone needs to eat. In the Bible, Jesus told people to share the bread, and he also multiplied the fish. His message was that one way to care for people is through food.

When I came to America as a young man, I thought the only religion in the world was Catholicism. I didn't know anything about the Jewish, Muslim, Mormon, or Buddhist religions, or any other religion. I was ignorant. But now, I'm curious about people's faith and believe that the more we know, the closer we can be to each other, the better we can care for one another. I dine with different people all the time and I like to ask them about their religion. I am fascinated by the range of beliefs, because at the end of the day, we are all more or less the same: We believe in the One and Only, our own God. There are a lot of good people in the world, of all religions.

When people aren't nourished, they can become hostile. It's understandable. We all know the feeling of irritability when we're hungry, but when that sensation never goes away it can drive a person to become embittered, despondent, and maybe even violent. It breaks my heart to think of children starting out in life that way.

What would happen if religious leaders sat down at least once a week to share a plate of pasta with people from outside their usual communities? And then what if those people did the same? Showing that you care by sharing a meal is a simple act and it could expand exponentially. Imagine all the religious leaders sitting around a big table with plates of warm, comforting pasta in front of them. One big family. They could talk about world peace while sharing the magical power and nourishment of pasta. That's my dream, and I'd like to be the one to cook the meal.

Pasta has the amazing power to bring people together.

When we left France we had no idea that we wouldn't be going back. In the beginning we stayed with my grandparents in their tiny house. They were our only grandparents, since my father was orphaned at the age of ten. We loved Nonno and Nonna very much, and they welcomed us into their home, even though they only had one bedroom for the adults and a little alcove where all seven of us kids slept. Despite how crowded it was, they encouraged us to stay, telling my parents that things were finally improving in Italy and it would be easier for them to find jobs. My parents were so relieved to be with family again after more than a decade that they immediately agreed. It wasn't the chance to make more money that decided it for them, but rather the chance to be surrounded by the love of family. Our return to Italy was a dream come true for them, but I had a lot to learn, first of all the language.

Mamma and Papa never wanted their children to know about their arguments, and so they didn't teach us Italian. We spoke French both at home and at school. Not that it saved us from witnessing things that no child should see—broken bottles littering the kitchen floor right after Mamma had finished scrubbing it on her hands and knees, a table thrown across the room because a piece of bread hadn't been fetched quickly enough, and bruises covering arms and legs after a particularly bad fight. We all lived in fear of my father's belt, but when he was in a good mood, he was the best. Today, I understand that many of my father's actions can probably be blamed on his growing up without parents.

At Italian school they started me out a year behind so I could catch up. Luckily I was a smart boy and learned quickly. With the help of my new friends and cousins, I adapted to our Italian life, although I've always felt as if I left a piece of my soul in France.

Things did improve for my family. We moved to San Bonifacio, a neighboring town, and lived in a small apartment. And after just a few years, my parents were given the opportunity to buy a small trattoria-style restaurant, including seven rooms upstairs for overnight guests. By then, my three older siblings were out of the house, and my younger brothers were still too young to work—which left me, at the age of fourteen, to help Mamma run Trattoria Cristallo. She did all the cooking and cleaning. I went to school in the mornings and then raced home to work as the busboy, waiter, bartender, and kitchen helper. We couldn't afford to hire extra help, so the two of us handled everything. Our workday often ended at two or three o'clock in the morning, many hours past a suitable bedtime for a young teenager.

Mamma was so open and caring toward our customers that Trattoria Cristallo quickly became a meeting place in the town. People chatted with me at the bar, where I did my schoolwork when there was a lull in my workload. I was one of the youngest bartenders in the north of Italy! People also came for Mamma's delicious classic Italian dishes like spaghetti with Bolognese sauce, homemade gnocchi, tortellini *in brodo*, and some of the French dishes she'd picked up over the years, such as French apple tarts, rabbit pâté, and duck à l'orange. One of my pleasures was watching her cook, putting love and passion into each dish, but I hated seeing her work so hard, seven days a week, eighteen hours a day, on top of being a mother of seven children and the wife of a difficult husband.

By the time I was sixteen it was too difficult for me to manage going to school and working late, so I dropped out. I look back now on my decision and can say that it's a shame I wasn't able to further my studies, but I was helping Mamma and don't regret it.

Mamma's advice about cooking pasta for the kids at the club has stretched into an unending series of tomorrows. I've gotten to know my young customers—who likes spaghetti best and who prefers penne, which ones are fast eaters and which ones take their time. Or so I thought. One afternoon I prepared a huge pot of pasta with broccoli for the kids. It's a dish I personally like very much, and the nutrition offered by the vegetable is good for growing children. They didn't eat it! At first I didn't understand why; then I quickly learned my lesson: Lots of boys and girls don't like green stuff on their plate. After that experience, I always blend the vegetables into the sauce so that they aren't visible. The veggies are there but the kids just can't see them!

Five o'clock has become a special time of the day. If I'm in town, I set aside the worries and problems of running a famous restaurant and relive the joy of mealtimes as a kid. Whenever I see a child with sauce smeared around his or her mouth, joking with friends between bites, living the single moment to its fullest, I remember when I was a boy and shared the same feelings with my siblings. Every afternoon I go to the club, I am reminded of my family and, through the kids, I have felt closer to Mamma and the rest of my family across a continent and on the other side of an ocean. Making sure these kids have a warm meal is not my dream—it's my mission.

Having fun being silly with the spaghetti (photo by Tony Zuppardo)

Mamma Caterina and baby Bruno

II

THE AMERICAN DREAM

"Do not neglect hospitality, for through it some have unknowingly entertained angels."

—HEBREWS 13:2

In 1976 my parents sold the trattoria. They had asked my opinion about whether or not to sell before I left, at the age of twenty, for my one year of obligatory Italian military service. I had no doubts. I had worked so hard for so many years that I told them I never wanted to see the restaurant again!

After years of Mamma running the trattoria, with Papa driving trucks, my parents were finally able to purchase their own home. Mamma raised rabbits and chickens in the backyard and took care of her garden. I remember I hated helping her clean the rabbit cages because of the disgusting smell, but she was thrilled to have her own little plot of land. They loved that house, and I was so proud of them for finally achieving something they'd dreamed of since the day they'd married.

When I concluded my service in the Italian Air Force, I found a job, with my brother's help, selling toilets. *Mamma mia*, I didn't even last twenty-four hours! In desperation, I ran to the first restaurant I could find and applied for a job as a waiter. They hired me on the spot. Several other jobs in restaurants followed—working up from waiter to maître d'—and eventually I was able to afford to live on my own in the beautiful city of Verona. I thought my life was

Bruno serving in the Italian Air Force in 1976

going well enough and, while I didn't have big plans yet for my future, I loved living in the city of Romeo and Juliette. And then one day my boss told me he had to close the restaurant. I felt like a collapsed soufflé.

Without a job, how was I going to pay the rent on the apartment I had just moved into?

My good friend Dino worked in a nice hotel in the center of the city and said that if I learned English he was sure I could get a job there, since—in addition to Italian—I was fluent in French. *What a great idea!* I thought. Maybe someday I could even get a job with an airline and travel around the world.

When I was still a kid, my sister Stella married an American GI named Fred and moved to Southern California. What better place for me to learn English? I had visited her for a month the year before, and I remembered how friendly everyone had been and the beautiful weather. I had no doubt that Stella would welcome me. It had been hard for her to leave her family behind when she married, and she'd confessed she still cried many nights because she missed us all. Back then, we did not have the luxury of Skype or email, and phone calls were too expensive to have more than once a week on Sundays. Italians feel lost when they don't have close contact with their family, preferably every day. It's not because they can't function without them, but rather that they feel the family gives them their identity. It's what helps them understand where they fit in the world.

Full of excitement for my new adventure, I began making the necessary preparations but avoided one important detail: I didn't tell my parents. I knew my father would try to dissuade me and that it would deepen Mamma's sorrow over already having one of her children on another continent. I finally told them, but Papa refused to speak to me until the day I left.

When it was time for me to go, Mamma kissed me, tears heavy in her eyes. She was sad, she told me, but happy that her daughter would have her younger brother there and wouldn't have to be alone. So typical of Mamma: Her kids always came first.

Bruno's first time in America circa 1980

By the time I boarded the plane for California in 1980, ready to learn English and more about the world, I had managed to save the equivalent of only two hundred American dollars. Fortunately, I had my sister and my brother-in-law waiting for me and offering me a comfortable bed and a plate of pasta. Stella refused to allow her baby brother to pay for rent or meals while I lived with them, and they generously took care of me in every way. Those initial weeks were like a dream: For the first time since I was fourteen, I had no job and no responsibilities, and I was free to enjoy the California sunshine.

I took long walks in Stella's neighborhood during the day. In the evening my nephew and niece patiently helped me as I struggled with English, and I listened to Barbara Streisand records in hopes of learning new words. After just two weeks I became anxious. I was accustomed to being around people all day long and was becoming bored.

Fred and Stella

"I want to get a job," I told Stella. I instinctually knew it would be the best way for me to learn English quickly.

The next day, she took me to several restaurants in the area, translating and helping me with the applications. The last place we visited was, as she explained, the best French restaurant in Orange County: La Vie en Rose. Stella spoke to the manager and explained that I was looking for a job as a waiter.

"He speaks French and Italian," she explained, "and a little English. He's a fast learner."

The manager shook his head. "I'd like to give him a chance, but I can't put him out front if he doesn't speak English. The only thing I can offer him until his English improves is a place as a dishwasher."

At the time I had no idea what the manager said and urged Stella to translate. She was too embarrassed to tell me. Her brother had been a maître d' in Italy, worked as personal waiter for a general in the Italian Air Force, had served the Pope's private pilot, and had spent years working in Italian restaurants. Washing dishes would be a huge step down, and she thought I would feel offended.

Instead, when she finally explained what the manager had said, I was elated. I could spend my days around other people in a beautiful restaurant and surrounded by delicious food. I didn't care if I washed dishes. I was just excited about having an opportunity to work in America. As it turned out, my lucky star was shining bright my first week on the job. One of the busboys quit, and the manager told me to take off my wet apron and start clearing tables.

Making my way around the dining room that evening, I felt as if I belonged. I used my best manners, worked tirelessly, and felt proud enough to burst at being part of such an elegant restaurant. I returned to washing dishes the next evening, but I didn't care. Hard work has never frightened me.

Learning the language proved to be almost harder than working long shifts in the restaurant, not having friends, and having to be totally dependent on my sister (even though she never complained and lent me her car whenever I needed to go to work). There were a number of people on staff at the restaurant—both in the kitchen and the dining room—who would have loved to see me fired for the mistakes I made, but the manager knew that not knowing English was my only weakness. I was a good worker and, for someone so young, knew a lot about the restaurant business.

One evening as I cleared one of my tables, I asked, "Was everything all right, madam?"

"Can I please have a doggy bag?" the woman replied.

I was furious. How dare she tell me to give the food to a dog! I stormed into the kitchen and threw the food in the garbage.

The waiter came in a moment later. "Bruno, have you got the doggy bag for table seventeen?"

"It is in the garbage. She told me to give it to the dog!"

The waiter started laughing. The steam of indignation rose within me, and my ears felt as if they were on fire. I did not like being laughed at.

When the waiter regained his composure, he explained what it really meant to request a doggy bag. For a split second I was relieved to know the customer had not offended the chef, but then I realized I'd made a horrible mistake. I swallowed the lump in my throat and tried to prepare myself mentally to be fired. How could I know that in America people took home the food they didn't eat when they went to a restaurant?

Fortunately, I didn't lose my job, mostly thanks to the customer and her husband who thought the mix-up was hilarious. They even left me an extra tip.

I could have easily been overcome by the humiliation of my ignorance. But growing up surrounded by other immigrant families like ours, everyone trying their best to learn the ways of the host country, I discovered that people from different cultures can see the world differently. Making a mistake about local customs is simply part of the integration process; another way of seeing things is not necessarily wrong. People are different and different is good, just like different ingredients come together to make a delicious dish.

After eight months in America, I had proven myself and could converse in English in the workplace. It was time to return to Italy. Even though I had been living with my sister, I missed my family, especially Mamma. I bought the cheapest ticket I could find on Pan American Airways and headed home.

When I arrived in San Bonifacio, the weather was horrible, the streets appeared small and dingy, and the people seemed rude. *Mamma mia!* What had happened while I was gone? The truth was that nothing had changed ... except me. I was happy to see Mamma and the rest of my family, but I couldn't shake the way I now saw my homeland.

Two weeks later, I was on a plane traveling back across the Atlantic.

Almost immediately after arriving in Los Angeles, I returned to La Vie en Rose. They rehired me, my English continued to improve (although some of my friends would say I've never really learned the language properly!), and they promoted me to waiter a short time later. Tableside flambé service, crepes Suzette, Caesar salad, beef tartar—I loved my job and I guess it showed. Requests for a table at "Bruno's station" became frequent. It felt like I was living in paradise.

After three years at La Vie en Rose, a new maître d' position was created, and they offered me the job. I couldn't believe my good luck. But it wasn't just luck; I had worked with all my passion since my first day on the job, and it paid off. I was the maître d' in a gorgeous French restaurant!

In 1983 I discovered that I still had a lot to learn. One night, a gentleman was eating dinner alone at table fourteen. He was very kind, and I thought he must be a businessman of some sort. Maybe he was away from his family and feeling lonely. I chatted with him to keep him company during his dinner. Since he spoke fluent French, we had a wonderful conversation. This man came in several times after that, and we always talked at great length, especially about the restaurant business.

Then one afternoon he approached me and said, "Hi, I'm the new owner."

I was shocked and a little frightened. The whole staff was worried about what was going to happen. Were we going to lose our jobs?

Instead, we were very fortunate because the new owner's goal was to take La Vie en Rose forward, to turn it into the best French restaurant in Southern California. I learned a life lesson from this experience: Always be careful when you are talking to someone you don't know. That person could turn out to be someone important. Thank goodness I'd been so cordial! He treated me as his right-hand man, and together we rebuilt the La Vie en Rose staff, the menu, and the style. He placed his trust in me, and I acquired self-confidence because I discovered I was ready to meet any challenge. I felt as if La Vie en Rose would be my home forever.

Then, two events occurred in 1986 that changed the course of my life.

The first was that I received the "Maître D' of the Year" award from the Southern California Restaurant Writers. Because of this recognition, people in the hospitality industry knew of my work and began calling me with job offers. I had no intention of quitting La Vie en Rose, but I went on a few interviews to be polite and keep my options open. One offer in particular, from a big-name hotel, was very tempting, and when I heard the salary, an intense throbbing started in my head. I had never held money in a position of high priority, but when I told my sister and her family about the offer, they all thought it was surely a good-enough reason to leave La Vie en Rose.

The pain in my head continued to torture me the next day when I went back to work. I had never suffered from such a headache. I decided to talk to my boss about my dilemma because, after all, I knew it was the cause of my pain.

Louis was honest and admitted that he could never match the hotel's offer. He also gave me some advice. He said that at the restaurant I was able to be myself, to be friendly and kind to all my customers, while at the hotel I'd just be one of several managers and essentially just a number. Me? A number? I couldn't get the thought out of my head. I asked for a couple of days to make a decision.

I decided to ask my soul what to do; the answer came to me quickly. How could I take the hotel job, prestigious as it was? Maybe I'd be making more money, but I'd be giving up so much more. The La Vie en Rose customers, my coworkers, and the restaurant itself were all like members of my family. I was born poor, and money was never a big part of my life, but family was important to me.

Bruno as a maître d', celebrating his first award with his brother, Eddie, and sister-in-law, Ornella; Jeri Wilson from the Souther California Restaurant Writers group is behind Bruno.

The other event occurred because I had made the decision to remain at La Vie en Rose. The maître d' from another restaurant came in for dinner one evening. As in any sector, people know each other, and since he was a colleague I provided his dinner for free. He offered to return the favor, and with my brother Eddie and his wife, Ornella, who were in town, we went to the restaurant where he worked: the White House Restaurant.

When I was about twenty feet from the front entrance to the restaurant, I stopped short. Eddie thought I was ill and that I was going to faint. But that wasn't it.

A strange warmth crept upwards from my toes all the way to my fingers, and I felt light-headed. What some people might call an out-of-body experience. The sensation began to dissipate, and I reassured my brother and sister-in-law that I was alright. We proceeded to walk inside the restaurant.

When I opened the front door, the first words that came to my lips were, "I would love to own this place."

As an Italian who has always enjoyed history and culture, I fell in love with the White House from the moment I saw it. The restaurant was located within a real house, built in 1909. It had been restored to maintain its original character, from the beautiful fireplace in the main dining room to the leaded glass windows and wooden flooring. And the staircase—oh, the staircase up to the second and third floors! I'd always loved how fresh and new everything was in California, but this house felt like coming home. My eyes roamed from the garden to each of the charming rooms and alcoves—and the wine cellar, too!

We had a lovely dinner, and later that year I returned with my parents and sister. I was in love, not with a person but with a place. La Vie en Rose was my first love, but once I saw the White House, something changed inside me. Love at first sight, like Mamma when she met Papa.

Then came my maître d' friend's phone call out of the blue. "The White House is for sale."

"That's nice," I replied casually, thinking nothing of it. "I hope someone good buys it."

My friend laughed. "I think it should be you."

I couldn't believe he thought I could afford such a thing. Although I had been working for seven years—often fourteen-hour days, seven days a week—life in Orange County was expensive, and my bank account held roughly the same two hundred dollars I'd originally brought with me to America.

"Just meet with the owner; he's a nice guy. Maybe you can work something out."

My financial situation was definitely an obstacle, and I was already aware that leaving the La Vie en Rose family would be heart-wrenching, but it wasn't the only thing holding me back. Was I really capable of owning and running my own restaurant? After all, I'd been a dishwasher just a few years before!

A few days later, I had a meeting with James Stovall, a construction worker who had bought the White House building with the intention of tearing it down to develop the land until his wife fell in love with the old house and talked him out of it. He was a big, intimidating guy, but our conversation remained friendly until it was time to talk about money.

"How much do you want for the restaurant?"

"One million," he said.

I felt so ashamed. Who did I think I was showing up there to discuss buying a restaurant? I may have felt successful in my own way but I was still a poor immigrant.

James must have seen the embarrassment on my face because he seemed to take pity on me. "Well, how much do you have?"

I just shook my head. "Nothing," I told him truthfully.

James stared at me for the longest thirty seconds of my life, as I wondered if he was going to throw me out or yell at me for wasting his time. Instead, he looked me in the eye and said, "I like your honesty." He held out his hand, and we shook. "I'm going to help you."

I walked out of the meeting with a deal to rent the restaurant from him for three years before securing a loan to conclude the purchase. I was equal parts elated and terrified.

When the time came to leave La Vie en Rose, where I had worked with true passion for seven years and had formed deep, lifelong friendships, I was sad but knew in my heart that I was making the right move. I cried when I had to say goodbye to Clementine Fuccinari, the "host with the most." She taught me so much from the very first day I walked in, until that last day I walked out. She is still one of my great friends.

The first weeks were hectic. I got to know the building, the staff, the menu, and the wine list. I would also eventually change the name to Anaheim White House Restaurant. Until then, the restaurant had served typical American cuisine, but I had different plans. I began by adding classic Italian dishes to the menu and spent the mornings teaching the chefs how to make Mamma's homemade gnocchi, polenta, and Bolognese sauce from fresh ingredients. I transformed the wine list, adding little-known Italian wines from northern Italy. However, the biggest change was in the presentation of the food, and it became one of our signature characteristics. We finished every plate with elaborate garnishes and whimsical touches—I loved seeing the surprise and delight on our customers' faces when the plates were set down on the table.

In addition to revamping the menu, the building needed attention. It was run-down and needed new furnishings, but all my funds were going toward paying the rent.

The first few months were terrifying. There were many evenings that my head waiter David, who'd worked with me at La Vie, and I stood out front on the porch waiting for patrons—who never came.

"Do you regret leaving?" he asked.

"White House Restaurant will be a hit, you'll see," I replied.

Maybe at the time I did have regrets, but the last thing I wanted to do was cause him to worry. An empty restaurant is a very scary thing, especially when there are bills to be paid. The long hours I spent at the restaurant, tirelessly doing whatever needed to be done, and often sleeping on the little sofa next to the front desk because I was too exhausted to drive home, were not much different from the life I led as a teen working at our Trattoria Cristallo. I hear people say that restaurateurs live the good life. They eat good food, drink good wine, it's one long party that never ends, they say. Boy, are they wrong.

A woman who claimed to be a psychic told me shortly after we opened White House Restaurant that there was a good ghost in the house. She said the ghost was an old lady wearing a slim, fitted gown, and she stood by the stairway with a whiskey in one hand and a cigarette in the other.

"Tell the owner," she said. "And don't worry, the ghost will love and protect him because he's going to do a lot of good. The restaurant will receive honors and publicity from all over the world. Presidents will dine here, and other famous people, too."

"I'll be sure to tell the owner," I assured her, while thinking she must be a crazy.

Bruno standing proudly in front of Anaheim White House Restaurant

(photo by Thierry Brouard / Prémium Paris)

White House is a landmark building so I supposed it was possible a ghost had taken up residence, but I had my doubts about where she'd gotten her ideas. Ironically, the psychic became one of the regulars at the restaurant for a short time—although I never saw the ghost—and I thank God that her predictions did come true!

Early on, my family swooped in to help me however they could. Stella lent a hand to clean the entire place from top to bottom and even took the curtains home to wash and iron them herself. My youngest brother, Freddy, and his best friend spent their California vacation cleaning out the wine cellar, and my sister Flavia passed on some of her most privileged home recipes like *Penne Amatriciana*. My vision was for customers to feel like cherished guests. I could feel my family's love and passion shining through every meal we served, and I hoped my guests felt it, too.

During those early years, I could only afford to call Mamma on Sunday mornings because it was so expensive. She understood that my life was taking shape in California and never complained that I didn't call often enough; knowing I was close to her oldest daughter, Stella, gave her peace. The funny thing is that when we were kids in France and we misbehaved, Mamma would threaten to send us far, far away. To a place that was so removed and so terrible that we would mend our ways. "If you don't behave, I'll send you to California!" she would yell. Mammas seem to know things before they really happen. We told her, jokingly, that it was her fault we were so far away now.

Anaheim White House at twilight (photo by Thierry Brouard / Prémium Paris)

When the three years were almost up, I tried bank after bank after bank to find a loan and, when everyone turned me down, I applied for a Small Business Administration loan, thinking it was my last resort. Two weeks before the final date set out in my contract with Jim Stovall, I received a reply from the SBA: I hadn't qualified. *Oh mamma....* If I didn't get a loan, I would lose everything—and after the countless hours of hard work, I couldn't bear the thought.

But fortunately there was a man rooting for me: Mr. Van Asperen, Vice President of the bank. He said he was trying hard to convince the SBA to approve my application, and in the end he succeeded. However, there was still one more obstacle. I had to have a Green Card. I had applied for one when I first arrived in America, but I didn't have the actual card yet, and I needed to have it in hand for the paperwork to go through. It was down to the eleventh hour, but there must have been an angel on my shoulder, because just a few days before the deadline, my Green Card arrived in the mail. *Mamma mia*, what stress! Finally, after so many hiccups, nothing could stop me from achieving my dreams of owning my own restaurant in America.

My hands trembled as I signed the paperwork for the huge loan. Later that day I splurged and called Mamma to tell her I was the president of the White House and that she was the First Lady. She laughed and asked if I'd been drinking.

The first time Mamma came to America and saw my restaurant, she danced up and down the stairs singing. Since her son owned it, she sang and felt it was hers, too. She was right—what is mine belongs to my family as well. A family shares what they have and takes care of one another.

My father gave himself credit for playing his role in the purchase. As he reasoned, he'd been the one who told me back in Italy that I wouldn't last a month in America. When I told him I was going to America, he'd felt offended that I didn't ask his opinion about making the trip, and I never forgot his dismissal. I yearned to prove him wrong and show him that I was strong enough to be in a foreign land far away from home. If it hadn't been for him, I would have been working a dead-end job in Italy.

(photo by Thierry Brouard / Prémium Paris)

Exterior shots of Anaheim White House Restaurant   (photo by Thierry Brouard / Prémium Paris)

The Abraham Lincoln Room   (photo by Thierry Brouard / Prémium Paris)

The Main Dining Room   (photo by Thierry Brouard / Prémium Paris)

33

Main dining room (photo by Thierry Brouard / Prémium Paris)

With time, word got out about the delicious menu and excellent service at Anaheim White House Restaurant and, despite the normal ups and downs of running a business, things were going well. However, the day eventually came when my maître d' David, my faithful friend and waiter who'd started with me in the beginning, left my employment. He and his wife wanted to raise a family, and the restaurant business often doesn't allow a person to participate in many of the important moments of a young family. There were many hugs and even more tears, but I knew that we would remain friends for life.

Now that David had moved on, I needed to find a trustworthy manager and maître d', but I knew it wouldn't be easy to find someone just like David. Eventually, I hired my nephew, Sylvano Ibay, even though he was young and had limited experience. The tradition of family working together is one of the cor-

The George Washington Room (photo by Thierry Brouard / Prémium Paris)

nerstones of Italian business practice, and I had no doubt about his dedication or that I could fully trust him. He has grown into the best restaurant manager I could ever ask for, and hiring him turned out to be one of the most intelligent business moves I've ever made.

I also got to know my community better in those early years. When I wasn't working or traveling, I was doing what I could to help a few of the charities in Anaheim. Little did I know then how much the Anaheim community would come to my aid many years later.

Shortly after I bought the restaurant, the Boys and Girls Club contacted me about donating catering services for their fundraising events. I've always believed in their good work with kids and was happy to support them. I've never forgotten how poor I was growing up, and interacting with the boys and girls helped me remember that, although times get tough, life has a lot of joyful moments.

One of the definitions of "home" is "the place in which one's affections are centered." Anaheim has been my home now for more than thirty years. During that time, I have grown to love the people and things that make Anaheim such a special place.

On my very first trip to California when I was nineteen years old, I couldn't wait to visit Disneyland. It was a place for dreams and magic, and I felt drawn to it like mozzarella to pizza. Little did I know back then that one day I would act as Grand Marshal in a Disneyland parade and work side-by-side with the organization to help needy children through programs at the Boys and Girls Clubs.

Sylvano and Bruno talking outside Anaheim White House

(photo by Thierry Brouard / Prémium Paris)

Indeed, through my involvement with the Boys and Girls Club and my work as a local restaurateur, in 2008 the City of Anaheim honored me with a star on the Anaheim Walk of Stars. I remember kneeling down near the plaque, surrounded by a group of smiling kids from the Club, and looking out at members of my family and my community as well as customers from the restaurant. I was there because of all of them. The star had my name on it, but it was theirs, too. The mayor even gave me the keys to the city of Anaheim last year. The only other person who has received them is the famous singer from Anaheim, Gwen Stefani. I feel so honored to be recognized alongside such a glamorous and wonderful person!

I also love Anaheim's professional sports teams: the Angels baseball and Ducks hockey. All I have to do is let the players know we've got a Caterina's Club event and they come to support and provide encouragement for the youth of Orange County. Their presence means a lot to the kids.

With all of Anaheim's wonderful organizations, caring people, and special individuals, I can't imagine having the restaurant anywhere else! So many special people contributed to making Anaheim White House Restaurant a top-class dining establishment, and I am eternally grateful for them all and their part in our success.

My Executive Chef, Eddie Meza, and I share a special bond through our individual experiences as immigrants to the United States, and we both know that through dedication and sacrifice it is possible to attain personal goals. He is a first-rate chef and I've been lucky to have him on my team.

Ghost or not, I've been blessed with the good fortune to have spent many years at Anaheim White House Restaurant. However, it is also thanks to the hard work and dedication of my staff over those years that it became so well known. We welcomed numerous famous guests and displayed photos of many of them in the restaurant.

For example, we had the pleasure of serving two US presidents. The first was President Jimmy Carter. The Secret Service checked up on all of us to make sure the restaurant was a suitable place for the president to have lunch, and we set aside the entire second floor for President Carter to talk about his new book. When he came in through the back door of the restaurant, escorted by Secret Service agents, I was very nervous and shook his hand.

"Welcome to the White House, Mr. President," I said, not intending to make a joke.

Also future President George W. Bush, who was Governor of Texas at the time, and his brother Jeb, when he was Governor of Florida, dined at the restaurant. He was very nice to all the crew, as was President Carter. *Mamma mia,* two presidents!

The list of high-profile celebrities who've dined at the Anaheim Whitehouse Restaurant is incredibly long, and it includes film and television stars, big-name athletes, singers, and so many others. Just to name a few: Gwen Stefani, Eva Gabor, WWE star Triple H and wife Stephanie McMahon, Naomi Judd, Suzanne Somers, Danny DeVito, Jamie Lee Curtis, Janet Leigh, Lionel Richie, Sidney Poitier, John Stamos, Doris Roberts, Jenny Craig, Keenen Ivory Wayans, soccer great Pelé, baseball slugger Barry Bonds, Derek Jeter, quarterback Dan Marino, the USA Volleyball team, Martina Navratilova, Italian tenor Andrea Bocelli, renowned chef Wolfgang Puck, astronaut Alan Shepard (who gave me the best review: "That was the best restaurant from Earth to the Moon!"), Dr. Leroy Chiao (who asked me to cater food to the space station), the Crown Prince of Belgium, photographer Greg Gorman, who is a frequent guest, and, finally, I did catering for Madonna.

I feel immense gratitude for the regular, loyal customers who followed me for more than thirty years. They all helped make Anaheim White House Restaurant the kind of place people cherished when they went out to eat.

III

THE MOTEL KIDS

"Bruno, I have been diagnosed with cancer, and going home instead
of to a motel room makes me feel so much better. Thank you."
—MARIA

The stress of not knowing if you'll have a place to sleep and something to eat
is like the stress of living in a war. And that war is called poverty. It's rag-
ing around many American families, and sometimes the difference between
getting caught in the crossfire or escaping with your life and that of your family
can seem random.

My chance to see firsthand what motel life is really like came one afternoon when a local news station wanted to do a piece about our Feeding the Kids
program. I knew the situation was going to be bad, but I could not believe my
eyes when I actually stepped out of the van with the film crew.

It was a beautiful Southern California day, but the cloudless blue sky and
piercing sun only highlighted the run-down nature of the motel, from the flick-
ering sign advertising hourly rates to the parking lot full of broken bottles, dis-
carded cigarettes, and telltale baggies that once held illegal drugs. Prostitutes,
dealers, and other shiftless characters loitered at the edges of the lot, while the
sounds of sirens and shouting hung in the air. I found some of the kids I knew
from the club playing on the cement stairs, right underneath a sign that read,

"Children prohibited from playing in this area." There was nowhere else for them to go. Somehow they looked smaller here than they did at the club, as if they'd shrunk against the harsh reality of their environment.

Hundreds of these motels were built in the mid-1950s to accommodate vacationing families drawn to newly constructed Southern California attractions by effective advertising, sunshine, and multilane freeways. Now, sixty years later, many of the motels are dilapidated and in general disrepair. Like most motels, the rooms have one or two double beds and a bathroom and no kitchen or cooking facilities.

The first family who opened their door to us had seven people living in the one tiny room. They slept two to a bed with three of the children on the floor. Their dirty clothes sat in the bathtub waiting to be washed, while the clean ones hung from the curtain rod. I didn't see food anywhere in the room, but that didn't stop cockroaches from scuttling about in hopes of finding a crumb.

Lucy, who I knew from the Boys and Girls Club, was the youngest in the family, and she showed us around. She was a spunky girl who liked school and was a good student. I asked her where she did her homework.

"My brothers and I take turns doing it on the toilet because it's the only quiet place here," she told me.

That afternoon was one of the early turning points for me, confirming that I had to do something that would make a lasting difference. As nice as a hot meal was, it still wasn't right for these kids and their families to be living in these circumstances, in on of the most dismal and dangerous of places imaginable. Lucy's mother and father both worked, but they couldn't save enough on their minimum-wage jobs to pay for the first and last months' rent on a house or apartment. I'd grown up with hard work and knew its value. We didn't have much, but as long as my parents were working, we could at least afford to have a roof over our heads and a plate of pasta to eat. These hardworking parents simply should not have been forced to raise their children in poverty, and it broke my heart to see them falling through the cracks in the system.

"Christina, can I speak with you privately, please?" I asked one of the servers working the weekend lunch shift.

She nodded, straightened her apron, and followed me into one of the dining rooms. I understand that the people who work for me might sometimes feel a little uncomfortable around The Boss, although I try to set a strong example of teamwork and mutual respect. I care about each and every one of my employees. Despite my attempts to be affable, Christina was clearly nervous. I invited her to sit down and I took a chair nearby.

"Why didn't you tell me you've been living in a motel?" I asked her.

Christina looked down at her hands clasped in her lap, and her long brown hair fell forward and hid her face.

"You already do so much," she said, her voice so soft I almost couldn't hear her. "I didn't want you to give me a job just because I live in a motel."

I saw her chin tremble and her shoulders round.

Her voice quivered. "Sorry, I'm trying not to cry."

She had been working for me for about three months, and in that time I had noticed her looking at me in a strange way. With a lot of emotion, as if I was the Statue of Liberty. Shy but desperately wanting to find the courage to speak to me. Tiptoeing around me. I'd never had an employee act that way and decided to ask my restaurant manager about her.

"Don't you know?" Sylvano had said. "Christina and her mom live in a motel."

It was as if I'd been punched in the stomach. I had absolutely no idea. My employees are like my family; how was it that I'd been in the dark about something so significant? I couldn't bear to think of her living in such difficult circumstances.

Sitting there in the silent dining room with her, my eyes filled with tears, too. It made me so sad to think of this diligent girl, who customers praised for her politeness and coworkers esteemed, living in squalor. I ached at the thought of her going home after work, not to a place where she could sit down to a nice meal and relax, but to a dangerous parking lot. I imagined her closing a cheap plywood door behind her, turning a rickety lock, and sliding a chain into place. I could see that she was trying to be so strong, but a motel is no place to grow up. She and her mother both worked; they deserved so much more.

"I read an article about everything you do for people who live in motels, and I dreamed of working for you. I was so happy when I got hired. I'm trying to help my mom save up so we can move somewhere else." She inhaled loudly. "Everything's such a struggle, and I just want to be able to think about my future."

I put my arm around her shoulders. I wanted her to know that she wasn't alone.

"I want to be like everybody else. I don't want people feeling sorry for me."

We both wiped our eyes and I fetched her a glass of water. Christina went on to tell me that when she was younger her parents separated, and she and her mother had to leave the house where she'd gown up because her mom couldn't afford to keep them there on her meager salary. She'd told her daughter it would only be for a little while until they found the right place for them to live. Weeks stretched into months. Even though her mom had a full-time job, they didn't qualify for any of the apartments for which she applied. At the time, Christina was still in school, and she told me it was especially hard when her classmates talked about college. She couldn't let herself think about the next month, let alone what she might want to do after graduation.

I still remember how Christina's voice shook and the tears in her eyes when she said, "I keep thinking to myself, how am I going to get ahead in life?"

The irony is that it's often cheaper to live in an apartment than a motel room. The cost of one-room motel accommodations without a kitchen can easily exceed the monthly rent for a decent apartment. Like so many other working families, Christina and her mom had moved into a motel because they'd come up against some hard luck and had no other options. That hard luck can take the form of a chronic illness in the family, a layoff, or, as in Christina's case, a divorce. Often some sort of credit problem follows. It is surprising how many great American families who've worked hard—dreaming of buying their own home—live in motels. It's usually their last option before becoming truly homeless and living on the street.

With no kitchen facilities, expensive convenience or take-out foods—which don't provide adequate nutrition—become daily fare. In turn, higher medical bills and obesity are frequent. To break the cycle, they have to come up with enough money to pay first and last months' rent and a security deposit, too, before moving somewhere more stable. For families living paycheck to paycheck, that extra money up front is like a brick wall so high that it blocks out the sun. The longer they stay in the motel, the harder it gets, and the more and more dangerous it is for the kids. Children who grow up around prostitution, drug deals, and gangs are more likely to be tempted by illegal activities, thinking they are the only options to escape the dilemma in which they live.

"We can get you into an apartment," I told her, thinking of the project Caterina's Club already had in place.

"No, Bruno, there are so many other families who need your help." Christina's long hair swayed as she shook her head.

I explained that it wasn't because she was my employee that I wanted to help, but that she qualified for our Welcome Home program because her residence was a motel.

"It's just me and my mom. We're saving up—you'll see. When I graduate I can work more and Mom hopes to get a better job too. Then we'll move out. Besides, you've already done so much for us by giving me a job." She stood up. "If you'll excuse me, I should get back to my station...."

I'd met other hardworking people determined to find a way to move and knew that fragile hope can easily shatter due to circumstances beyond a person's control. Christina's selflessness was amazing, and it made me want to give her a hand all the more. Several days later, she and I talked again about their situation, and I finally convinced her that Caterina's Club could help. Within days, they moved into a two-bedroom apartment not far from her school. Christina graduated and continued to work at the restaurant for some months. I was sad when she left to live in another state but was hopeful for her future.

Whenever one of my employees moves on with his or her life and steps up to new challenges, I always have bittersweet emotions. I wish them all the best, but like an old-style Italian parent, I also wish they could stay with me forever. I've watched them grow up, and when they leave, it's like they're leaving home.

Christina stopped by the restaurant last year to say hello. Unfortunately, I wasn't there at the time, but Sylvano phoned me when she was in his office.

"Give her a hug from me," I said. "And tell her that if she wants to come back to work for us, the door is always open."

In fact, she has since returned to work part-time at Anaheim White House, and I couldn't be happier. It's a pleasure to have her among us.

Christina and her mom weren't, however, the first family we helped.

We started the Welcome Home project in 2012 so that families could finally escape the vicious loop of paying weekly rent in a motel. For our program, qualifying families need to have at least two children, one parent needs to have a full-time job and have held it for at least six months, and they must be able to afford the rent for the apartment of their choice. They also need to be clean in terms of drugs and legal problems. Holding down a job is proof a person wants to be back on track. We calculate that about 75 percent of the men and women living in motels in our area have jobs, many of which pay minimum wage, and after paying weekly motel rent there's just not enough left over to save up for a deposit on an apartment. So, we give them the boost they need: first and last months' rent and the security deposit. It makes a huge difference for the family when they can move into safe, stable surroundings. When the kids see their new home for the first time, it makes me feel so proud, and I know Mamma would be proud, too.

The first family we helped through the project was a mother, father, and five children. They had been living in a single motel room for twelve years. Twelve years! The three youngest children had lived in the motel since birth. They didn't know what it was like to live anywhere else. When I saw them again several years after they'd gotten out of the motel, I noticed that the two oldest children—teenagers now—were smiling. I'd never seen them smile before. Not once. They were different kids now that they truly had a place to call home.

I remember another family that qualified and moved into a townhouse on two floors. The family had six children, and when the kids saw their new home they couldn't believe it was all for them. Everyone had their own bed to sleep in! The kids were thrilled about the carpeted stairs, too. They'd never lived in a house that had its own stairs. They climbed up and slid down, giggling the whole time. I love that sound! It reminds me of the games my brothers and I played together. We didn't have carpeted stairs, but we did like to laugh.

When a family gets out of a motel, it means the kids get away from the bad environment and can feel safe. Studies have found that homelessness and motel living cause very real stress in developing children, and the constant worry that they will have no place to live takes a significant toll on them. Getting into a stable home helps parents recover their dignity, too. And with a kitchen, they can prepare healthy food for the kids, like pasta. *Viva la pasta!*

IV

HEROES—BIG AND SMALL

"Ask and it will be given to you."—JESUS

In 2009 and 2010 I lost 40 percent of my business, but I wasn't alone; I saw people all around me lose their jobs and houses because of the economic recession. Some of these people were customers, and some were neighbors and friends. It was easy to understand why our dining rooms at the restaurant were sometimes empty.

One day, my head chef and my restaurant manager approached me. They needed to speak with me, they said. When we sat down in Sylvano's office, their faces were grim.

"We're having trouble paying the bills," Sylvano began. "We can't keep going like this. We haven't got enough paying customers to cover costs for the restaurant and the charity. Something's got to give."

I had never stopped to figure how much we were spending for the motel kids, but Sylvano showed me the numbers: It was costing $30,000 to $40,000 a year. I'm not sure how, but in some way I had covered the expense. I came from a poor family, I'd bought the restaurant with no money down, and I was carrying what amounted to a lifetime mortgage. I am not a rich man, but somehow I'd supported our meal program all on my own. However, I couldn't spare the money anymore if I wanted to keep the restaurant open.

But I couldn't stop making pasta for the kids. How could I? My heart split in two at the thought of hungry children without their pasta dinners. What would I tell Mamma?

The same week Mike Baker called from the club. "We have a problem," he said.

I gasped. *Oh no, is the pasta overcooked? Has there been food poisoning?*

"The number of kids is growing every day. Is there any way you can double the amount of pasta?" he asked.

I felt torn in two directions: My beloved restaurant was in serious jeopardy, but those children needed me. Together they—the restaurant and the kids—were my heart and soul: One couldn't exist without the other. I didn't know then that both of these things would be in far greater jeopardy many years later. Somehow I'll make do, I told myself, just like Mamma always did when the number of place settings at the table increased at the last minute.

I remembered how she'd make room for another plate on the table—for a schoolmate or a friend from the neighborhood, or perhaps for someone passing through—and add extra pasta to the pot. And if there was a little less food on our plates, the conversation around the table made up for it.

My parents couldn't afford to buy what peddlers offered, but Papa always invited them to share a meal. Having been orphaned at the age of ten and, on his own, forced to take care of his younger brothers and sisters, he understood what it meant to be hungry. When he ran out of money, he took his siblings to live on the streets, where he sold anything he could find in order to keep them from starving. He knew the hardship of being turned away and the importance of remembering where you came from. I'm grateful to him for instilling these values in me.

As I fell into bed the night after Mike's appeal, I said an extra prayer. Doubling the quantity was going to be a real challenge. *Mamma mia*, what was I going to do? I *had* to make pasta for those kids.

When I arrived at the restaurant the next day, I told Sylvano that we weren't cancelling the pasta; we were doubling it. Then I called Mike.

"Tell the kids there's enough pasta for anyone who's hungry," I said.

The important thing was that the children knew someone cared and that they benefited from the love I poured into every pot. I was sharing Mamma's love with them. What could be more important?

Up until then, I'd been cooking about twenty-five pounds of pasta and three gallons of sauce every evening. It was enough to feed about one hundred fifty kids. In less than a month, there were three hundred hungry children. And the numbers continued to increase every week.

I refinanced the loans on my house and the restaurant to keep everything afloat. Many evenings we had very few paying customers at the restaurant—in fact, there were many days that the number of hungry children we fed exceeded the number of paying customers—but knowing that we had served all those kids made my heart feel better, although the pressure was building. My family and my staff all thought I was crazy, and maybe I was. But deep down I knew something would save us. . . .

Around this same time, we added a new wing to the restaurant. We already had a banquet room on the second floor but needed larger facilities for corporate events and weddings. Although I had no experience with construction, I knew that I didn't want to deal with dust and noise for months. A few friends helped design the addition, and we broke ground in early spring with plans to have it complete before the holiday season. People kept telling me that there was no way I'd have it finished in such a short period of time, but I've never let the naysayers hold me back. Their comments only made me work harder.

We sent out invitations for the grand opening of what we call the West Wing, even though, ironically, it's located on our east lawn. I wanted to make this part of the restaurant as gorgeous as the real White House and also wanted to maintain the look and style of our landmark building. The event was scheduled for November 2, 2009.

Shortly after we mailed out the invitations, the city requested a meeting with my construction workers and me. After a brief discussion, they told me that our opening date would have to be pushed back because the permit would not be ready by then, and without a permit we could not open the new wing. The people from the city didn't know me very well: I had four hundred people invited for a 5:30 p.m. event. I could not back out.

I slept badly the night before the grand opening. All day, I sweated and felt on the verge of panic as I greeted our lunch customers with a tight smile and showed them the big red bow I was going to cut in a few hours' time. I was afraid someone from the city would show up and tell me they were shutting down the event, but I couldn't allow my fear to stop me.

With little more than an hour to spare, I received a phone call from the city. I'd gotten my permit! What timing, what a relief. Maybe the ghost had helped me again!

What I didn't know at the time was that we were in the middle of the worst recession America would ever know since the Great Depression. Things were not looking good at all. Our sales dropped dramatically, and in 2008–2009 we lost a lot of our customers. I felt like I was on board the Titanic after it hit the iceberg. It's a good thing I had my life jacket on—the West Wing Banquet Room.

Five years later, all the construction costs had been paid off with the help of a friend, and as a result of the increased number of banquets and weddings we were able to host. Recession or no recession, the desire for romance survives. Times continued to be tough, but we all worked hard to keep our ship seaworthy. The restaurant would make it . . . but what about the kids?

God heard my prayers for guidance, and on August 9, 2010, a miracle occurred.

It was three o'clock in the afternoon, and I was at the restaurant. There were only a few other employees there with me, since the evening shift didn't start for another hour. The phones started ringing, all seven lines at the same

The new West Wing for banquets and weddings (photo by Thierry Brouard / Prémium Paris)

time. People were calling from the East Coast of the United States to ask what they could do to help feed the kids. About an hour later calls began arriving from the Midwest, and finally calls came in from the West Coast, too.

I had been contacted by *CBS Evening News* the previous month. The caller told me Katie Couric had heard about what I was doing for the motel kids and wanted to air a segment about it. They flew Steve Hartman out to interview

The new West Wing for banquets and weddings (photo by Thierry Brouard / Prémium Paris)

me, and I'd been happy to tell him about what we were doing. It wasn't the first time I told the story of Caterina's Club, and after the interview and filming were over, we all returned to business as usual. I've always known that media attention can help spread the word, but I had no idea the segment would cause an avalanche of help. And there was an amazing follow-up too: Katie Couric did another story about us a week later, but that this time we were prepared, and I had employees ready to answer the phones. About half of the calls were from media outlets wanting to interview me, and the other half were from regular people across the country asking how they could donate to our program.

Six years after the first plate of pasta was served, we suddenly began receiving donations. I was overwhelmed by the generosity of so many kind people and grateful it came just at the point I had exhausted all my resources and was beginning to lose hope that I could continue feeding the kids. If I'd been forced to make that decision, I would have been devastated.

Letters poured in, too. One was from a nine-year-old girl in New York who sent me her ten-dollar allowance. I cried when I read her letter. Another was from a senior citizen who sent five dollars and wrote that she didn't have much money because she was surviving only on her social security, but she was giving all she could afford. I cried again. A waitress from the Midwest wrote that she'd had a terrible day serving rude customers and thought it was possibly the worst day of her life until she watched the story about us on Katie Couric's program. She sent me the tips she'd earned that day: sixty-five dollars and a few cents. Again I cried.

When we received an anonymous donation of $50,000, my heart overflowed. All those people were showing me how much they cared and that I was not alone. Each and every single gesture of kindness touched me and, more important, it was the kids who benefited from such generosity. It's not about how much you give but how much love you put into giving.

I was flooded with requests for interviews. I didn't care about personal publicity, but I saw that with each printed article or broadcast more support arrived for Caterina's Club. Within a few months, *People Magazine* chose me as one of their heroes of the week, and Bill Handel of KFI AM 640 radio interviewed me and spoke about the motel kids. People sent money or asked how they could help, and awareness about the difficult situation these children were facing every day quickly grew and grew. Caterina's Club was making a difference in a bigger sphere.

And at home, many wonderful people remain supportive of Caterina's Club.

Vicki Gunvalson and Mira Sorvino

Paul Sorvino

Actor Joe Mantegna

At home, many wonderful people remain supportive of Caterina's Club and volunteer to help with the daily meals served to the children.

Back home in Italy with the family for one of Mamma's birthdays

By this time, Mamma's Parkinson's had progressed to such a degree that she was no longer able to make her annual trip to visit Stella and me in California. We continued to Skype every single morning, even though her speech was becoming affected by the disease, too. I returned to Italy to visit her whenever I could. I'd take her for a spin in her wheelchair in the main piazza of San Bonifacio, a soft blue blanket tucked in to keep her warm, or to sit down for lunch with her and the rest of the family like we did when we were young, or I'd bathe her and help her with her medications and put her to bed. Caring for her brought me such joy, yet moments of happiness are often mixed with sorrow. For example, it was during this time that my sixteen-year-old cousin, Andrea, was killed in a road accident. *You went to heaven too soon, but they needed you up there. Ciao, Andrea.*

Being far away from my family has been the most difficult part of my life. However, over the years I've been able to make a number of surprise visits, and they've always been fun. One Christmas I hid inside a giant box dressed up as Santa Claus. The whole family was gathered at my sister-in-law Ornella's for Christmas dinner, and she presented her special gift to them. They began tearing at the wrapping and opened the box. I popped out but didn't say a word. Ornella's gift, they agreed, was indeed original, but they quickly moved on to other gifts and the meal. No one recognized me for thirty minutes! When one of my brothers finally pulled off my fake beard, tears welled up in Mamma's eyes and she hugged me tight.

"Oh, *caro*, the best Christmas present ever."

Each time Stella or I visited Mamma, her joy and love were so profound that words are not adequate. Her face resembled that of a pure, blissful angel.

After the coverage on CBS, it seemed that the newspapers, magazines, and television and radio stations finally understood that reporting on stories about the bad economy isn't what changes things; actions are key. And people like to hear about them. With the arrival of donations, we were able to continue delivering pasta without interruption. I breathed a huge sigh of relief.

Spending my evenings serving pasta and getting high-fives, chatting with the kids and beginning to know them better, and watching them grow and play in a safe environment was the high point of each day. I had exceeded Mamma's expectations, but I still felt like I wasn't doing enough for the motel kids.

Some of the boys and girls came to the club wearing the same clothes day after day and month after month, long after they were torn, soiled, or outgrown. For those few hours after school, they could run and play and be kids, but I knew that the contrast between the club and their home lives was enormous. It bothered me to know that even though their stomachs were full, they still had to return to a crowded motel room.

"I live in a motel with my grandma, my mom, my sister, my brother, my other little brother, a newborn baby that's coming, and my aunt. I sleep on the floor. My mom tells us we can't go outside and play. We have to stay with the door locked until she gets home because it's not safe. There are people in the parking lot who sell drugs and sometimes the police come," one of the boys told me.

There had to be something more I could do.

In 2011 I received a phone call I never could have dreamed of, not in a thousand years. The person on the other end of the line told me he was calling from CNN in Atlanta and that I'd been chosen as one of the twenty-five CNN heroes for the year. Me? A hero? I thought one of my friends was playing a crazy joke on me, like when I got the call to cater for Madonna. ("Yeah, right," I'd responded, but that call wasn't a joke either.) I soon understood the caller from CNN was bona fide.

One of twenty-five people chosen from all over the world! What a blessing to be recognized alongside so many amazing men and women. I was delighted that news about Caterina's Club was about to reach even farther afield and, hopefully, that we could continue to do more and more for the kids. I felt I was living a dream.

September 22nd was Mamma's birthday, and it was also the day CNN would announce the selection of the network's ten finalists—from the original list of twenty-five—for their Hero of the Year. Could two of what felt like the most fortuitous events in my life be somehow linked?

I woke up at dawn, knowing that the names of the top ten candidates would be made public in the early morning. I did my best to wait patiently, but I fear I failed miserably. I anxiously opened and closed cupboard doors, rearranged furniture, sat down and then stood up again.

Anderson Cooper began to read the list. As I listened, I felt detached from my surroundings but at the same time intensely aware of every cell in my body. "... Bruno Serato. Caterina's Club..." *Oh, mio dio!* I could hardly believe it was true.

Later, I called home to Italy via Skype, where my brothers and sisters, together with Papa, were with Mamma celebrating her 87th birthday. I wanted to share with them the feelings of anticipation and excitement that I'd felt earlier, so when their faces appeared on the screen, I told them to wait for just a moment because I wanted to check to see if my name was on the top ten list. (Good thing they didn't know the announcement had been taped hours earlier.)

"Well, everybody," I said, when I returned in front of the screen with a somber face, "the important thing is that today in Mamma's birthday. Let's focus on that celebration."

They all looked disappointed, and I even noticed a few teary eyes. We turned our attention to singing "Happy Birthday" to Mamma, and they cut the cake.

After half an hour, I couldn't hold it in any longer.

"I actually have something to tell you all," I said, my voice somber.

"What, Bruno?" someone asked with a touch of trepidation.

"You may want to sit down for this one ..." I held my voice steady. They all looked worried.

Then I shouted at the top of my lungs, "We're in the top ten!" Their shocked faces and joyful reactions were worth the wait.

"*Vai all'inferno,*" my brothers exclaimed, through their smiles. *Go to hell.* "How could you lead us on for so long?"

"I'm going to heaven!" I told them, "Not hell." In a matter of seconds, the tears and champagne began to flow.

I knew, unfortunately, that Mamma and Papa wouldn't be able to attend the award ceremony that was scheduled to take place in December. They had grown too old and frail to travel. However, I insisted that my four brothers and two sisters accompany me to the event. I wanted them in the audience with me to share what I felt would be one of the greatest evenings of my life. All seven of us had never been in the United States together before, and it meant so much to me to have their support. I told them that they would be my guests, and that if they refused my invitation, I'd never speak to them again.

In the two months leading up to the event, I was walking on cloud nine and busier than I'd ever been. The attention surrounding my selection attracted more donations for Caterina's Club and more publicity for our mission. CNN asked me to make a video about what we do and the children we serve, to discuss my origins, the Boys and Girls Clubs in Orange County, and the underlying problem of poverty and hunger in America. They asked me to prepare a short speech. I did my best to write a powerful and authentic message.

My brothers and sisters arrived three days before the big event. I picked them up at the airport, and we went straight to the Boys and Girls Club where Caterina's Club began. After twenty hours of travel, they helped serve pasta. It was a joyous moment together with my siblings, and we celebrated the same hearty food we'd grown up eating by sharing it with the kids. Mamma wasn't there in body, but she filled the room—and every stomach—with her spirit.

Mamma and Papa were in Italy with their caregivers; it was the first time one of us was not close by. We all prayed that everything back home would go smoothly.

On the morning of the ceremony, December 11th, I woke up with the energy of Superman. Poverty and hunger among children were my archrivals, and I was determined to defeat them.

Festivities at the Shrine Auditorium in Santa Monica began at 3:00 p.m. I wore a handsome, tailored Italian suit and walked down the red carpet three times just to breathe in its magic.

Susan Sarandon came up to me and said, "I know who you are—you're the chef who's feeding kids!"

Chef Bruno with Freddy, Sylvano, Stella, Flavia, Eddie, and Corrado, serving pasta at the Boys and Girls Club (photo by Albert Evangelista Photography)

I couldn't believe that she knew who I was. I watched the other candidates take their trip on the red carpet too, and I had to wonder how I could be so lucky to be in their company. They had dedicated their entire lives to making a difference in the world through their inventive and compassionate causes. I couldn't help but feel a sense of humility and awe in their presence.

When it was time to enter the auditorium, proverbial butterflies fluttered in my stomach. I led my sisters to their seats in the front row—my younger sister on my right and my elder sister on my left. Our brothers were seated directly behind us. This was the first time they witnessed me being honored. I had received other awards, but there was always a void in my heart as I accepted them because my family was back home in Italy and unable to share the moment. We embraced one another, our emotion just barely below the surface. Five thousand people filled the hall, including movie stars and other famous people, and I remember thinking: These are the *real* Oscars. We're not actors in a film, and the stories we're about to hear are *true* reality shows. (If they ever make a movie about my life, I'm hoping Brad Pitt will play the role of Bruno.)

In recognition of their tireless work and dedication, the other nine heroes from 2011 include:

- Eddie Canales, Gridiron Heroes (emotional and financial support to high school football players who've sustained life-changing spinal cord injuries);
- Taryn Davis, American Widow Project (support for young US military widows);
- Sal Dimiceli, The Time Is Now To Help (assistance through food, rent, utilities, and other necessities to people in need);
- Derreck Kayongo, Global Soap Project (recovery and reprocessing of used hotel soap for needy communities worldwide);
- Diane Latiker, Kids Off the Block (helping young people avoid gang violence);
- Robin Lim, Bumi Sehat health clinics (providing free prenatal care, birthing services, and medical aid in Indonesia);

- Patrice Millet, FONDAPS (educating children in Haiti through sports to become responsible citizens);
- Richard St. Denis, World Access Project (providing wheelchairs and mobility aids to people with disabilities in rural Mexico);
- Amy Stokes, Infinite Family (connecting South African children affected by HIV/AIDS with teenage "net buddies" from all over the world via the Internet).

After the first candidate was presented, I leaned close to my sister and said, "I hope he's the winner. He's doing so much good."

And then I repeated the same words as each of the other candidates took the stage. I considered myself the smallest and least worthy of all. There was a need, my mother suggested I do something about it, and I did.

When Jerry Seinfeld—a phenomenal actor, a true comedian, and an endearing gentleman—began speaking about Caterina's Club, my heart felt like it was beating at two thousand miles per hour. It wasn't that I was nervous; my emotions were soaring at the thought of friends, family, and customers watching me all over the world—in other parts of the US and in Italy, Japan, Australia, and France. When I stepped onto the stage and bowed with a flourish, it was my own personal way to thank them for their support.

"I want to feed the kids all over the world, but before I do that, I want to feed the kids right here in America," I began. "We should not have hungry kids in our own backyard."

CNN had told me to keep going even if the audience applauded after the word "America." They feared I might not be able to finish my speech. They also told me to follow the teleprompter, but I didn't even know where it was! I just spoke from my heart.

To conclude, I said, "It is time to stop talking about it, but to do something about it." Then, I shouted, "Ciao, Mamma!"

Even though her health had deteriorated significantly by then, and she had lost her ability to speak, I knew she and Papa had their television on in Italy and that her expressive eyes and loving smile were there for me.

Then I heard my youngest brother call out from the audience, "Brunooooo!" And I called back, "Ciao, Freddy!" just before I left the stage.

The whole evening was amazing. Apart from the glamour, excitement, and publicity, we received a generous donation from CNN for Caterina's Club and thousands of encouraging messages filled my personal telephone. Our heroes— the children who battle hunger every day—were the ones who had been honored, and we continue our efforts to help them grow up into caring adults.

Chef Bruno with his 2011 CNN Heroes Award (photo by Jeremy Freeman/CNN)

Chef Bruno Serato with comedian Jerry Seinfeld   (photo by Jeremy Freeman/CNN)

Napoleon Hill once said, "Strength and growth come only through continuous effort and struggle." Recognition from CNN was not an end-point: I continue to work hard even now to see Caterina's Club reach its full potential.

Many people believe that since I've been on CNN and appear in the media I must be rich and the restaurant must be full every night. That is not the case. Like anyone else, I have to budget and calculate each month in order to pay my mortgage. My philosophy has always been that money should never be a priority in one's life, as my parents taught me when they decided to move the family from France back to Italy because of family relationships, not money.

Two weeks after the CNN award ceremony, Papa died. It was a shock because I had called via Skype just two days earlier and saw him dancing around the house, seemingly in good spirits and health. He simply laid down for a nap and never woke up. I got the call at 4:00 a.m. When I heard the phone ring, I thought to myself, "Mamma! Is she okay?" But Freddy explained that it was Papa, not Mamma, who we had always expected to go first because of her Parkinson's. It was an awful day for me, but I thanked God that he'd gone so peacefully. We all knew Mamma couldn't bear the loss of her husband of sixty-five years and we agreed we would not to tell her. In spite of his temper, which improved once we had all grown up, they had a powerful romance and Mamma loved him so much. In the last two years of his life, he gave her all of the love and attention she had always wanted from him. She lived out her last few years thinking her great love was living in a hospital under special care. Although in her heart, she knew.

I left for the funeral in Italy as soon as I could.

While I was there, I showed Mamma the video of my speech at the CNN event. I held her hand as we watched the last four seconds—"Ciao, Mamma!"—over and over, searching her face for some sign that she understood. Mamma had lost her speech because of her Parkinson's disease, so her only form of communication was from facial expressions and her hand. Finally, after about the tenth time, she squeezed my hand tightly—three or four times in rapid succession—and tears came to her eyes while a smile lit her face. *Grazie, Dio.* She'd understood!

"It's all because of you, Mamma," I whispered in her ear, as my own tears rolled down my cheeks.

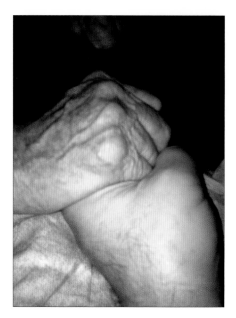

Bruno holding Mamma Caterina's hand

Papa, Bruno, and Mamma Caterina (photograph © Greg Gorman)

V

THE PASTATHON

"How can you not help kids who are hungry and want to eat?"
—BILL HANDEL, RADIO TALK SHOW HOST, KFI AM 640

I was walking on the beach with a friend when my cell phone buzzed with an incoming message. *Anthony has been named student of the month at his school! Thank you, Bruno.* I stopped in my tracks. My feet refused to move, the joy I felt was so intense.

Anthony's family was the second we helped move from a motel. His father had left his mom and their three kids at Christmastime and, with nowhere else to go, they had relocated to a motel. They'd been living there for more than a year. Anthony was a wonderful twelve-year-old boy with lively green eyes and a bright mind, but he was struggling at school. In fact, he was close to being expelled. His little sister Tara told me one afternoon when I was at the Boys and Girls Club that she didn't have any friends because she was too embarrassed to let anyone see where she lived. These were great kids and I'd felt such sorrow, knowing that at their young age they had to face problems that even an adult would find overwhelming.

Studies have shown that children can't learn if they're hungry. Add to that the stress of being essentially one step away from homelessness, living week to week in a motel. The impact on children is devastating. Not surprising, we see proof day after day that getting a warm, nutritious meal every evening and living in a safe, stable environment can transform a child who may seem to be going nowhere. When kids eat better and get out of the motel environment, their school work and behavior improve. The Boys and Girls Club is also a huge asset. There, kids can find help with homework and a suitable environment where they can play, develop social skills, and embrace their childhood.

When Anthony's mother sent me the text message, they'd been living in a new apartment for several months. His academic improvement was dramatic in the most wonderful of ways. He was learning how to interact with his classmates and complete his homework on time, and he was making constant progress.

For his birthday that year, Anthony told his mother that his greatest wish was to cook for Chef Bruno. He said he'd eaten so many of my meals that he wanted to have a chance to cook for me. When I found out, I invited him to the restaurant kitchen for a cooking lesson. The first thing I did was put a chef's hat on his head. It was too big and kept slipping down over his green eyes, but it couldn't cover his smile. While the other chefs prepared the lobster, shrimp, and calamari for the restaurant seafood platter; the stuffed giant tortellini with fresh filling; and rolled chicken breasts with ham, porcini mushrooms, and local mozzarella for that night's specials, I taught Anthony how to make Mamma's classic tomato sauce. The same sauce that had kept me warm on the coldest days of my childhood. It was an honor to share it with Anthony, as it is with every child who eats my pasta.

When we were done cooking, we carried out the giant dish of spaghetti, and in one of the White House private dining rooms, we sat down to eat with the rest of Anthony's family. Anthony's proud smile was radiant, especially when his brother and sister complimented him on the pasta. His mother's appreciative expression was priceless.

As we sat there—Anthony, his family, and I—enjoying the meal Anthony had prepared, I couldn't help but think of Billy, whose potato-chip dinner inspired all of this. Here was a family that had faced some of the worst moments possible, a boy who was on the brink of being cast aside by the education system and a little girl who'd excluded herself from friendships because of her sense of humiliation; yet with a bit of loving support they had overcome the obstacles.

Mamma had been right: Pasta was the first step. The simplicity of pasta sets the groundwork for small moments of joy and connection when we look at each other over a meal and recognize we're all human beings with a responsibility— as well as the privilege—to care for one another.

In my own country of Italy, there is a huge problem with unemployment for young people, even for those who have university degrees. My best advice for them, or anyone facing what seems like an enormous obstacle, is don't give up. There have been so many times when a part of me thought I couldn't go on—at the Trattoria Cristallo, as a dishwasher at La Vie en Rose, as the new owner of Anaheim White House Restaurant, in the worst moments of the economic crisis when bills and hungry children seemed to grow every day—but enduring that moment of doubt is crucial. Perseverance leads to success. And never stop helping others who are less fortunate. We can all look around and see people who are worse off than we are. I tell young people today that if they don't have monetary resources, they can give someone a smile or a hug. It can mean so much to a person, and you'll see that you will receive something as well. It costs zero dollars to be a decent human being.

One of my favorite no-cost gestures was to say hello to strangers as I pushed Mamma around San Bonifacio in her wheelchair. It became an essential part of every day when I visited.

It was barely noon on November 13, 2015, and the equivalent of a male African bush elephant—15,000 pounds—was already piled up like a mountain on the lawn of the restaurant. The amount of pasta and sauce multiplied as the donations poured in. By evening, it looked like a small herd of pachyderms was crowded in front of the restaurant, and collection continued until 10:00 p.m.!

Once a year, Burbank California radio station KFI AM 640, one of the most popular radio stations in the country, hosts a radiothon to collect donations for Caterina's Club in the form of pasta, tomato sauce, and cash. Everyone at the radio station—the crew, the executive producer, Michelle Kube Kelly, and the station's well-known radio personalities Bill Handel, John and Ken, and Tim Conway Jr.—have generously adopted Caterina's Club as their favorite charity. Each of them places the same amount of love they have for their own mother or father into the project. The station broadcasts from the banquet room at the restaurant and donors come with their hands full and their hearts even fuller. We welcome them all and appreciate their thoughtfulness. All that love and kindness for the kids and the families touches me so deeply that for days I feel an inner glow. As of this writing, more than one million dollars and 150,000 pounds of pasta and sauce have been collected for the cause through what has become affectionately known as the "pastathon."

The donations collected over the past five years during the event have made it possible for us to expand Caterina's Club meals to thirty-five different locations in seventeen cities in Orange County, serving Boys and Girls Clubs, Section 8 families, and deliveries of uncooked pasta and ready-to-serve sauce to several trailer parks. In order to get the food to those in need, we rely on four employees who cook the pasta and the kind drivers who make the deliveries. We now serve almost two thousand kids a day, which entails cooking eighty pounds of pasta and forty gallons of tomato sauce every day. It takes approximately eight hours each day to prep, cook, and clean everything. In addition to supporting Caterina's Club, the radiothon funds are the main financial source for our Welcome Home project. There are not enough words or gestures to convey my gratitude.

People come bearing grocery bags full of spaghetti, car trunks loaded with cans of tomato sauce, and $10 or $20 bills; children with piggy banks; school groups with hundreds of pounds of pasta; and local business owners with donations. I can't express how much I appreciate everyone's support and how much it means to me when someone stops by, gives me a hug, donates what he or she can, and tells me his or her own story—perhaps of living in a motel, and what a difference a program like Caterina's Club or the Welcome Home project could have made in his or her life.

Once a lawyer told me that she'd been a motel kid. She said that every day her mother told her to lock the flimsy, battered door to their room and to never go outside unless she was with her. I embraced this now distinguished-looking woman and told her to give her mother a kiss from me. She had done her best by keeping her safe.

Another time, a guy contacted me and asked if he could bring in some pasta to the restaurant to donate. Of course, no need to ask! Some weeks later on a Saturday afternoon, I heard the roar of one hundred motorcycle engines in my parking lot. Really loud motorcycle engines. When I went outside, I saw a bunch of Harley bikers in leather jackets and chains. *Mamma mia*, what was going on??? *Thank goodness the restaurant wasn't open yet,* I thought, *otherwise my customers might run away!* I shouldn't have been so quick to judge.

The guys donated 1,200 pounds of pasta for the motel kids. To thank them, I invited them inside for a glass of champagne.

As we got to talking, the biker who had called me explained that when he heard about my program, he knew he had to help. He'd once been a motel kid himself.

When I asked if he came from a poor family, he said, "No, Bruno. My parents were drug addicts and dealers. Many nights I didn't have dinner because the only thing my parents cared about was getting high. I never saw food on the table, only drugs. I ran away when I was sixteen."

The man was covered in tattoos and chains and, to tell the truth, looked pretty scary. But when he told me he wished there'd been a Chef Bruno back when he was a kid, I asked him if I could give him a hug. (It didn't seem like a good idea without asking.) I'll never forget our embrace.

Although the lawyer and the biker aren't, as far as I know, acquainted, they know a lot about each other. And there are thousands and thousands—maybe millions by now—of people who, unfortunately, can understand their childhood experiences. However, you don't have to be a former motel kid to be empathetic or generous. All it takes is to open your heart.

I'm elated about the number of people who reach out to contribute to our cause. However, I am sometimes frustrated by a lack—on the part of some Boys and Girls Club directors who seem to be annoyed by our involvement—to proactively combat the problem of hunger because it is seen as a hassle, even though we do all of the real work involved. I see the kids, I talk with the families, and I read the statistics. My heart aches for the children who are not getting enough to eat and for the hard-working families who just can't get a step ahead. I want to see this beast—hunger—eradicated. The roots pulled out, like a weed in a vegetable garden.

The problem isn't a lack of food on a global scale; it's a lack of distribution. I'm not minimizing the efforts of those who support Caterina's Club, or all the others who have started their own charities to meet the needs of children who suffer from poverty, or individuals who share what they have when they encounter someone who is hungry, but I am saying WE HAVE TO WORK TOGETHER! Only through collaboration will we put food on the table for all the children who otherwise go without.

The United States Department of Agriculture has, for many years, run meal programs for children from low-income families. For example, the National School Lunch and School Breakfast programs are crucial to assure the nutrition these children need to learn, play, and grow. The USDA has another program—the Summer Food Service Program (SFSP)—that helps feed children throughout the summer who normally rely on morning and midday meals at school. The SFSP usually provides one or two meals per day at various sites, which may be communities where incomes are well below the poverty level or at organized summer activity centers or camps. Currently there are more than 47,000 thousand sites throughout the United States, serving about 2.5 million children. All three of these programs help immensely to fight hunger among children. However, I disagree with the quantities of food mandated by the nutritional guidelines.

According to the SFSP meal pattern for children ages six through twelve, lunch or supper should be composed of: 1 cup of 1 percent or nonfat milk as a beverage; ¾ cup of vegetable or fruit (two or more kinds), half of which may be full-strength fruit or vegetable juice; one serving of grains or bread, which is defined as 1 slice of bread or ½ cup cooked pasta, noodles, rice, or similar; and one serving of meat or meat alternate, which is defined as 2 ounces of lean meat, poultry, fish, or cheese, one egg, ½ cup cooked dry legumes, 4 tablespoons peanut butter, 1 ounce nuts, or 1 cup yogurt. Reading this list gives the impression of an adequate meal; certainly it is balanced. But when you put it on a plate for an active, growing child, it does not seem like enough, particularly if it has to last the child fifteen hours on weeknights and maybe even for an entire weekend. Motel children generally do not have access to a kitchen stocked with food, and many of them receive only two meals a day. It doesn't seem right that these kids spend their summers—a time for fun and recreation—with a gnawing, empty feeling in their stomachs.

For this reason, Caterina's Club is proposing an initiative project in 2017 to our government in Washington to develop new guidelines with larger portions and more flexibility for evening meal patterns in hopes that the findings will lead to changes in federal policy. Our annual pastathon provides us with the funds we so desperately need to expand our reach and ensure that more children obtain the food they need to learn and grow—and live happy, healthy lives.

VI

LIFE IS A COMBINATION OF MAGIC AND PASTA[1]

"Everything you see I owe to spaghetti."–SOPHIA LOREN

"Bruno Serato?"

"Yes?"

"I'm calling from Barilla."

Barilla is the best-known pasta producer in Italy and perhaps the world. The pasta in the blue box. An image came to mind: smiling, laughing, happy children, a smear of tomato sauce on a smooth chin, fork gripped in a small hand, the last bite lifted from an empty plate.

The caller explained that someone at headquarters had seen me on an Italian television talk show speaking about Caterina's Club, and they were so touched they urged the Barilla family to make a donation. I hadn't even made a request, and they took the initiative to offer their help. Amazing! What a beautiful surprise—but the real surprise was yet to come.

About fifteen days later a truck arrived with tons of pasta and tomato sauce. An entire truckload, full of pasta and tomato sauce for my kids. My vision blurred and I reached into my pocket for a handkerchief. The shelves in our storeroom were getting bare, and their donation came at just the right time.

---

1 A quote from film director Federico Fellini.

With their support we would be able to feed thousands of hungry kids. The supplies lasted six months, and Barilla told me that if I ever ran short to let them know. Their act of generosity was more than I could have ever dreamed of, and their amazing support continues. At the time I didn't have any personal connection to Barilla—I'd never met anyone from the company—and yet they believed in what we were doing and offered their assistance. It was extraordinary.

The best way to fully understand the kids' enthusiasm and love is to spend time with them. To listen to them, to laugh with them as strands of spaghetti with tomato sauce hang out of their mouths, to play with them, to provide an example.

When kids welcome me at the club with a high-five or a story about school, I feel such gratitude. They are my joy, and caring for them gives meaning to my life. In Italy, children are the light in the eyes of parents, grandparents, aunts, and uncles. I can never forget the sense of belonging I felt when we returned to live surrounded by family in Italy, and I want to share that love with children who have challenges to face that are bigger than they are. I can't work miracles—I'm just a drop in a bucket—but I try to do my part.

In 2012 I was in Las Vegas, where I gave a speech at the Western conference of the Boys and Girls Clubs of America, after having received the President's Volunteer Service Award from Barack Obama. During my speech I encouraged the representatives of the clubs to follow the example of our program of feeding pasta to hungry kids, to reach out to their local restaurants for support, to call me for help. Just imagine, I told them, what we can do if we work together. It really costs so little to make a plate of pasta. The money that only one customer pays for a restaurant meal can feed twenty, thirty, or more hungry children. The fact that no one who was present on that day contacted me was a disappointment, but it didn't stop me. I continue on my mission to feed hungry boys and girls and won't rest until there are no more children going to bed with an empty stomach.

Since Barilla had been so generous with our program in California, I asked if the company would be willing to support similar programs at Boys and Girls Clubs in Brooklyn and Chicago, with the aim of providing the kids with a pasta meal once a week and fostering healthy lifestyles. Pasta is a cornerstone of the Mediterranean diet, an approach to food and eating that can help prevent chronic diseases and that promotes well-being. Without delay, again Barilla lent a hand.

It was an emotional day for me when I visited the Brooklyn Madison Square Boys and Girls Club. I watched as three hundred boys and girls ate delicious, wholesome pasta, generously donated by a company based on another continent, as an outgrowth of Mamma's simple idea during a visit to me in California. A web of loving ties between caring individuals that extended around the world, consolidating a deep and tangible sense of family—a family that reaches beyond its own home to embrace, to nurture, and to rejoice in shared experiences.

I also visited the Barilla Academy restaurant in New York and, approximately a year later, gave a speech at Barilla headquarters in Parma, Italy, about how the company's generosity and dedication to helping the greater community, especially through their Share the Table movement, are making a difference in the world. On both occasions I was struck and deeply touched by how the people working for the company embodied that same sense of one big, caring family. My respect for the Barilla family and their commitment to the power of pasta is unending.

Thanks to Barilla's outstanding example, other producers of pasta and sauce have come forward to join us in our mission, including Pastificio di Martino Gaetano, New World Pasta-Ronzoni, and Pastificio Felicetti. Many of the generous donations have been facilitated by the president of the Italian Pasta-makers Association, Riccardo Felicetti, and distributed by Ciba California. It is refreshing to witness such large corporations taking social responsibility. Corporate generosity is helping us make a difference for so many children who will grow up to be the caretakers of society in future decades. In Italian there is the saying, one hand washes the other, and together they wash the face.

Many of the children who eat my pasta are faced with problems that go beyond the scope of normal childhood. I pray that through the pasta they eat, they know they are cared for and that the world isn't all bad. But I know that pasta alone can't solve all their problems.

One day, a young teen who came to the club regularly disappeared. The first day Eastone didn't arrive, no one worried particularly, but by the third day the director was extremely concerned. The young woman never disappeared like that. When she finally showed up, she was dirty and hungry. When we asked her what had happened, she said that her father told her he could no longer afford to pay for their motel room and that she was on her own. She slept on a park bench for two nights until a friend helped her get back to the club, where she knew she would find warm food and people who cared. The club made the necessary phone calls and found her a foster family.

These kids desperately need our help. While pasta isn't the only thing they need, it surely helps, as does a hug and an adult who knows what to do.

One time, a little girl came up to me after a lunch we'd organized at the restaurant for the kids.

"Chef Bruno," she said, "can you write a letter to my mom that says I can come back to this restaurant whenever I want?"

I smiled. "Of course. It's a pleasure to have you."

My friend Fifi Chao was standing nearby and overheard our conversation. Tears began to well in her eyes. Afterwards she said, "You know why she asked you that, don't you? She feels secure here with you, Bruno. She needs to know that this is a place where she's welcome and that it won't be taken away from her."

I too wiped away a tear. That little girl and all the other kids like her deserve to know that there is more to life than a motel room and a parking lot. They need to know that something better is waiting for them.

One evening I was talking to a boy at the Boys and Girls Club. When I asked him where he lived, he turned bright red. Later, his friend told me that he lived in a garage across the street. The boy was almost in tears when he knew I'd found out. I searched for the right words to say to him, and got the help I needed from someone above.

"Have you got a roof over your head?" I asked.

He nodded.

"When it rains, do you get dripped on?"

He shook his head.

"Well, I have a friend who lives in a garage, and every time it rains he says the garage turns into a swimming pool. And he doesn't know how to swim!"

The little boy's blue eyes crinkled up and he started to laugh. He tilted his blond head back and his mouth opened wide with laughter. Sharing laughter is just about as wonderful as sharing pasta.

One of the incredible things about pasta is that it's versatile. It can be served with almost any type of sauce or vegetables, with or without meat or fish. It suits almost everyone's taste and it's filling and inexpensive to prepare. When combined with a sauce based on vegetables or legumes, it provides important fiber, vitamins, and minerals.

Pasta is one of the basic building blocks of people who live in the Mediterranean, a wholesome and delicious approach to eating that, according to some nutritionists, is an excellent way to promote good health and favor bio-cultural diversity. Most people in Italy consume pasta on a daily basis. The tradition of family or extended family meals is an integral part of Italian culture, and also of other countries around the Mediterranean basin. Memories created around the table are among the strongest. If you close your eyes and think of a special Thanksgiving or birthday meal for example, I'll bet you can recall tiny details of the setting, the people, and the food. These memories are lasting, and by setting positive examples around the table at mealtime, we hope—through partnership with Barilla's Share the Table movement—to instill healthy values, camaraderie, responsibility, and confidence in the daily lives of the children we serve.

Taking time out of the day to eat a proper meal and share conversation with friends or family supports emotional health, and eating together strengthens the relationships between people and favors good digestion, too. Consuming prepackaged meals or convenience foods alone or in front of the television means missing out on friendship and shared moments, and it can lead to a sense of isolation. It has been said that pasta is more than a food—it's a philosophy of life. And I couldn't agree more!

Another reason behind pasta's power is that it is a sustainable food. What I mean by this is that the production of pasta has less impact on the environment compared to many other foods. For example, food life cycle assessments indicate that pasta—from harvesting the durum wheat to production of pasta to preparation at home and package disposal—has a carbon footprint of only 14.5 oz/CO2eq/lb, making it a so-called low-emission food. Research has shown that grains like the wheat used to make pasta use only about a half a liter of water to produce one calorie of food. In addition, pasta is more energy dense than fruits and vegetables, and it discourages waste because leftovers, such as vegetables, meats, or cheese, can be used to create delicious dishes, especially with the addition of healthful ingredients like olive oil. Other facts that make pasta special include its ease of handling and it's light weight, that it doesn't need refrigeration, and its packaging is completely recyclable. When you consider all of these aspects, it's no wonder that pasta, in various forms, is found and enjoyed throughout the world.

I always try to use products that are as natural as possible and of good quality, and frequently I add meat or fish and/or vegetables or legumes to the pasta sauce as a way to include the various food groups in a single, easy-to-prepare dish. I've never found a child who categorically says they don't like pasta. That is, with the exception of my nephew, Alberto Serato! It's hard to believe that my own nephew, whom I adore dearly, is the only kid I know who doesn't like it, but it's the truth. However, on my last visit to Italy, Alberto, with a big smirk, said, "Uncle Bruno, I have big news for you . . . I've started eating pasta once in a while. Just be happy with that, okay?"

Regional dishes made with pasta or noodles can be found worldwide. Pasta is a global food. Consider that people in China cook pasta-like noodles in woks, *fideos* are popular in Spain, children in Japan—as in Italy—eat a form of pasta at school, in Thailand noodles are an important ingredient in many traditional dishes, and that in North African couscous is made from the same type of flour, but is worked into grains rather than rolled out into various shapes like pasta.

Through the Boys and Girls Clubs, we've facilitated meal programs in Chicago, Texas, New York City, and Mexico, although some directors insist on keeping the pasta limited to one day a week. I always ask them the same question: Do children need a warm, nutritious dinner only once a week?

One Boys and Girls Club director told me he wanted to stop serving pasta because he said it was making the kids fat.

"Strange," I told him, "yours is the only club that has this problem. Maybe your kids need more physical activity?"

Overly processed and fast foods, sodas, exaggerated portions (especially with regard to desserts), and a lack of physical activity are the primary culprits of obesity—not pasta with freshly prepared sauce or vegetables. A proper portion of pasta will never cause obesity. Thankfully, some of the Boys and Girls Club directors are welcoming our program with smiling faces and happiness for the kids. They are the directors that we love.

Michelle Obama contributed to fighting obesity and supporting a healthy diet through her "Let's Move!" campaign aimed at children by furthering knowledge about food and exercise. I commend her efforts, but we still have many children who are not getting adequate amounts of healthy carbohydrates and protein.

Athletes know how important carbohydrates are for their diet. The Internet is full of meal plans and suggested recipes for pre-race or training, and pasta is almost always one of the stars. Children who play and go to school need energy, too!

In addition to the many individual athletes who have come to my restaurant, I have fed entire teams as well. In 2005, the US men's volleyball team relocated their training center to Anaheim and began coming to the restaurant five days a week for post-practice lunch. My agreement with the team was that I would feed them well for the next three years, until the Olympic Games in Beijing. But if they did not come home with the gold medal, I would give them all food poisoning! I got very close to the team, and some of the players turned out to be great friends. The years passed and they went through some really tough qualifying matches, and finally, it was lunchtime on the day before their departure for China. There was a lot of emotion and many hugs.

During the semifinal match I was glued to the screen, watching every play. I was waiting for my sister and brother to return from a trip, and the moment they walked in the door, our team scored the winning point. I screamed so loudly that Stella and Corrado thought someone was attacking me. But, instead, I was just a happy man.

On the evening of the final, I was a guest for dinner at the home of the former Anaheim mayor, Curt Pringle, along with Stanley Cup winner Joe Di Penta and his wife Jessica. I was trying to be very polite during the meal, but I suffered through each minute, not knowing how the match was progressing. Curt was also anxious to know how it was going, and he finally placed a laptop on the table. We all burst with pride and celebration when the match was over.

The Anaheim Ducks ice hockey team have also been frequent guests, and many of the historic players are close friends. This coming together of physical activity, good wholesome food, and personal interaction fits the needs of the athlete as well as engaged members of society.

One reason that pasta is a healthy food is that it has a low glycemic index, especially when it's cooked properly—al dente. This means that, because it is digested slowly, it produces gradual rises in blood sugar and insulin levels, rather than producing a sudden peak as do foods with a high index. Remember, pasta that is overcooked has a higher glycemic index. In other words, properly prepared pasta, combined with the right kind of sauce, is like a timed-release

Lidia Bastianich, wonderful cookbook author, restaurateur, and host of the
popular TV show *Lidia's Kitchen* dons a Caterina's Club apron to prepare food with me.

tablet: It provides energy and nutrients to the body slowly, over a longer period of time.

In addition, there is a phenomenon called "the second meal concept" in which the sensation of feeling satiated for a prolonged period after consuming a pasta-based meal carries over to the subsequent meal as well. Scientists have concluded that, in addition to being weight-control allies by helping to curb appetite and delaying hunger, foods with a low glycemic index may decrease the risk of developing diabetes and cardiovascular disease.

So when someone says that pasta is fattening, I have to strongly disagree. Children in Italy have traditionally eaten pasta at lunch or dinner, as well as fresh-made, quality pizza—avoiding junk food—and they are rarely over-weight. Only in recent years, with the introduction of American-style fast and junk food, have weight problems begun to appear among Italian children and teens. Plus, many of the people who appear to gain weight from eating pasta are actually consuming too many servings or ordering pasta dishes that are laden with cheese and heavy cream sauces. Italian mothers and grandmothers know that pasta is an important food for growing children and adults alike, and they encourage the people they love to eat it. "Mangia, mangia!"

All I know is that pasta truly is magic for the children in Caterina's Club.

VII

THE HOSPITALITY ACADEMY

"It is time to stop talking about it, but to do something about it."
—CHEF BRUNO

A fifteen-year-old boy at the Boys and Girls Club came up to me and asked, "Chef Bruno, can I work for you?"

"Sorry, but we serve alcohol at the restaurant, and so I can't have you work in the dining room," I said. "But when you're eighteen come talk to me." I handed him my card with my number on it.

Three years later he reappeared and pulled the card out of his pocket. It was crumpled and half torn.

"Chef Bruno, do you remember me? I'm Jose. You told me that you'd give me a job when I'm eighteen years old. Well, today is my birthday!"

We were at the height of the economic crisis and I'd suspended all hiring. The restaurant was barely keeping its head above water; we were on the brink of closing. Yet I couldn't bring myself to not hire him. His face was so full of happiness and hope because now he was old enough to work. I hired him as a busboy on the spot. Jose worked at the restaurant for about a year. He was a hard worker and I was sorry to see him move away to another city with his family, but it had been a pleasure to have him on our team.

When I look at the young people who have started their working life, especially the dishwashers, at White House Restaurant, I'm filled with emotion. That was me, thirty-five years ago—struggling to keep up with the pace, hoping to move up the ladder, falling into bed at the end of a long shift. Maybe some of them will become owners of a restaurant one day like I have. They can't see it yet—it will take unending dedication and a sizable dose of good luck—but it is possible. I'm filled with hope for their future.

In February, 2016, we launched a program that I've been dreaming about for a long time: the Chef Bruno Hospitality Academy. In collaboration with the Anaheim School District Mentorship Program, this twelve-week course is the first Hospitality Academy in the nation for students in grades seven to twelve. Each semester, twenty-five students can explore every angle of the food service industry through hands-on instruction: food preparation and nutrition, cuisine, restaurant service, marketing, administration, and customer service. But everyone in the program starts out learning how to wash dishes. Our aim is not only to teach skills but also to offer a unique and lasting experience that includes mentorship and networking for future employment. We want to keep teens in our community off the streets and involved in activities that will help shape their future and provide them with opportunities.

Watching our students grow and learn week to week is amazing. They are so inspiring. In the beginning they are a little afraid and insecure, shy but full of desire, and as they progress, they gain confidence and skill. I'm cheering for each one of them. We have already made a commitment to take on four of the students as interns at the end of the course, and we are striving to place the others in local food service businesses. In 2017 we plan to double the size of the class, and we have already hired two kids from this program. I was lucky enough to learn about working in a restaurant under Mamma's watchful eye at the trattoria, and I am privileged to help raise the next generation of chefs, restaurant staff, and future leaders. Restaurants are important focal points in every community, and by teaching young people about the industry we hope to encourage independence and innovation, to maintain traditions, and to help instill the value of giving back to society through service.

One of the most remarkable accomplishments of Caterina's Club is that it has served as an example in other countries. Our charity has been show-cased on Univision, a Spanish-language network, and similar organizations have sprung up in Latin America. In addition, Antonella Clerici, television host of the most popular cooking show in Italy, invited me to be on her program a couple of years ago and surprised me by revealing that she too was starting a program to feed hungry kids.

Also, in Italy, there are now four secondary schools in the northern town of Ferrara where students participate in our Power of Pasta campaign thanks to

Antonella Clerici hosts her popular Italian television show *La provo del cuoco*

my friend Gabriele Lumi. When, at the kick-off event, I stood in front of the students who attend schools that specialize in a restaurant and hospitality curriculum to tell them my story and about the motel kids and their families, I could feel the contagion spread of wanting to help. As a result of my presentation, the schools set up "Power of Pasta" displays and collection points and coordinated with local charities to cook and distribute the pasta to needy families. When people understand what a difference their small gestures can make, they catch a disease I call the "virus of good." And in the case of young people, who are full of compassion and a desire to make a difference in the world, their involvement and enthusiasm spread like the delicious smell of a lovingly prepared home-cooked meal.

It makes me so happy when someone comes to me about starting a meal program in their own city or country. It's Mamma's love reaching wider and wider! I always knew she had a big heart. "Name your own program after your mother," I always suggest when people say they want to follow the Caterina's Club model. I can't think of a better way to build a monument to maternal love, that unending force of nature.

I am aware that many generous people dream of giving back to their communities but simply don't know where to start. It's not difficult to copy my project. All you have to do is take action, rather than just talk about it.

I encourage people who want to make a difference to follow my few simple steps. When I started out, I didn't have any idea where I was going and so I didn't always do things in the most efficient way. But the results are what are important!

The first step I suggest is to write a mission statement. Consider things like what your charity will be called, its purpose, and your goals in the short- and long-term. It's important to visualize the future so you can recognize what it can and will achieve. For example, my goal is to make sure that all the impoverished kids in the world have enough nutritious food to eat.

The next step is to promote your charity. Attend as many events as you can where there will be people who can support you. Network with other organizations, use social media, and contact local newspapers and radio stations. And since you already have a clear mission statement, you can share your vision more easily with others.

The fiscal aspects of a running a charity can be complicated. If you are operating in the US, apply for 501(c)(3) status. This permits your charity to be recognized as such and therefore your organization is tax-exempt, with the understanding that you will not personally profit from your charity. It may take two or three years for your application to be processed and approved, so don't delay. Most countries have a similar tax status for nonprofit, charitable organizations. Another important step is to join with a fiscal sponsor. A fiscal sponsor has 501(c)(3) status itself and, generally for a fee, also sponsors other organizations that may not yet have the means or the approval to run their charity independently. Good fiscal sponsors provide financial advice, will most likely manage several charities, and will encourage your organization's independence. I recommend that you maintain your relationship with your fiscal sponsor for a few months beyond the time your charity receives its own 501(c)(3) status so they can help you get started on the right track. Your charity will also need a lawyer or certified public accountant once you're on your own. Because the Internal Revenue Service has strict rules and regulations for charities, I suggest you select a professional who has experience in this area. A lawyer will help protect you from any potential lawsuits and can advise you on insurance coverage for your organization.

One of the legal requirements for a charity is that you need an executive board that will meet regularly, adhere to the by-laws of the organization, and vote regarding issues pertaining to the charity. These are typically pro bono positions in which members volunteer their time and advice because they are passionate about your cause. When you search for people to be on your executive board, I advise you to include one or two members who are well acquainted with you and your philanthropic interests. It breaks my heart when I hear about individuals who get pushed out of their own charities!

The final organizational step is to set up an advisory board. These are people who will not vote on matters that arise, but they will provide you with valuable advice and will work to promote your charity. Their positions are also voluntary. Choose members who are respected leaders in the community, who have interest in the work you do, and who can reach out to various subgroups. Having people with a variety of professional and personal backgrounds makes it easier to reach a larger slice of your community.

Starting a charity requires dedication and hard work, like everything else in life that has value. But I can assure you that when you see the smiles of the people your charity has touched, every last struggle is worth it. If you have the heart and the passion, you can do it, and you will quickly learn that with your success comes the success of so many others.

Over the years, I have made my mistakes, but I have learned from those experiences, and here are my pieces of wisdom:

- Never give up.

- Respect your friends.

- Always listen.

- Ask for help when you need it.

- Never forget where you came from.

- Take time to talk with others.

- Do something you're passionate about.

- Thank people every day.

- . . . and, of course, love your Mamma!

VIII

KIND WORDS ARE
THE MUSIC OF THE WORLD

"Be kind whenever possible. It is always possible."
—DALAI LAMA

Some months after I ran into Billy, the boy who started it all with his potato chips, I received this letter:

Dear Bruno,

Meeting your mom for the first time changed my life, but I didn't know it when I was seven. I remember I was at the Boys and Girls Club, playing with my friends that afternoon. I was hungry and so I ate some potato chips and noticed two adults approach me. Not knowing who they were, I stayed quiet but noticed they seemed concerned about what I was eating. The sweet old lady said something to the man, who asked me if that was going to fill my stomach for the day. I nodded my head. The lady spoke to the man in a language I didn't really under-stand and then they left.

About an hour later, they came with a tray of food. I didn't know what kind of food it was, but it smelled good and it was hot and ready to eat. The man approached me and with an accent said something like, "Hey, little boy, this is my mom, Caterina. My name's Bruno. We've brought pasta for the kids at the club." We all ate the pasta since some of us wouldn't get a hot meal at home. Caterina and Bruno left the club with big smiles on their faces. The next day, Caterina and Bruno came back again with more pasta. I wanted to ask Caterina why she came back, but she didn't speak English. Caterina and Bruno brought pasta to the club every day, and Caterina took some pictures with our club girls.

Ten years went by and I spotted Bruno serving pasta at the Boys and Girls Club again. When I approached him, I asked him if he remembered me. Bruno, laughing, said, "Should I?" "Yeah, because I was one of the first kids to try your pasta!" Bruno was shocked and came and hugged me hard. He said he wanted my family and me to come to his restaurant. When we got there, Bruno got to meet all my family and told them our meal was on the house, that we didn't have to pay for anything. When we were getting ready to leave the restaurant, my family saw pictures of Caterina and Bruno. My sister was real surprised when she noticed she was in one of the pictures, sitting right next to Bruno's mom. When we told him, Bruno was so glad and he hugged my sister.

For my sister and me to be part of something important makes us happy cause we know there's a lot of kids who have a hard life. It's great that Caterina's legacy will continue as long as you keep serving pasta every day for all the kids.

Thank you, Bruno. Thank you, Caterina.

Billy

It warms my heart to hear from the people Caterina's Club has touched. Below are a few more of the extraordinary letters I have received:

> "Bruno, my grandkids were motel kids a couple of years ago and because of your help and support their family has moved forward and are all doing great. You provided the help they needed to find success and for that I thank you very much! You are an amazing person."

> "Now only if we had two versions of Mr. Serato in every major city, what a difference it would make! I hope everyone who reads this story goes beyond just commenting here on 'what a nice guy Mr. Serato is' or 'ah, that's nice' and actually get inspired to do something worthwhile to help some family near them crawl out of this dark hole."

> "Chef Bruno, I am not embarrassed to invite my friends over to play anymore! Thank you for helping us get our new home. I love it!"

One evening after having worked a typical fifteen-hour day, I read the following message from a girl who has been eating my pasta for seven years. It makes all the hard work worth it:

> "These are my grades from 1st semester [copy of report card] and now I got student of the month and High Honors for a 4.0 GPA. Thank you, Bruno."

Toward the end of 2015, I received a call from a woman named Carolina. About a year ago, she and her husband, together with their two children, had qualified for our Welcome Home project. They'd chosen a nice two-bedroom apartment they could afford, and the kids quickly settled in to their new home. Now that they had a kitchen, Carolina told me, the children asked her to make pasta all the time. She then shared her big news—that she'd just given birth to a baby girl and wanted to let me know that she'd named her Caterina.

How can I express the joy I felt? Tears rolled down my cheeks as I held the phone in my trembling hand, and the memory of Mamma's special smell was so real it seemed she was there in the room. "Pure" is the only word I can find to describe it. Soft and clean, like something pristine and uncontaminated, just like her love.

When I told Carolina that I wanted to include a piece about her family in this book, here's what she wrote:

> When I hear the name Bruno, it doesn't even have to be followed by Serato. I am reminded of a man I never even knew existed until February 2014 when my family and I had fallen on hard times and we were living in a motel.
>
> My oldest was seven years old and was in second grade. She had to do her homework sometimes on the floor. It broke my heart to see her writing on the floor of the motel room. My youngest at the time was only three years old. She wasn't in school yet but was very aware of what was going on around us. Thank God we weren't in the motel very long compared to some other people, but for me . . . every day felt like an eternity. It was then I got to know who Bruno Serato really is.
>
> We had started attending a church service on Sundays at the motel where we were staying, because sometimes we didn't even have enough for gas to go to the church where we usually attended. It was there at the motel church that someone referred us to a club called Caterina's Club. Only God knew what an impact Caterina's Club would have on our life.
>
> Because of Bruno and Caterina's Club we were able to leave the motel and move into our own two-bedroom apartment, which we called Our Palace. When I first met Bruno, I had no idea HE was Bruno. He seemed very casual and interested in our story of why we were there.

The process went by so quickly it felt like a dream. Within three days we were in Our Very Own Palace. It was AMAZING!!! Between Bruno and his assistant, Kaylee, our world had been turned around completely. Even after our move, we kept in contact with Caterina's Club. Always remembering how it changed our life forever.

A little after a year I found out we were expecting our third daughter. It was unanimous—her name would be Caterina. In honor of Bruno's mother and Caterina's Club. We are forever grateful for Bruno, his staff, his life, and his passion to help families have an opportunity to get out of what could be one of the worst situations a family could live through.

These people's stories and courage are a huge part of what keeps me going every day. Each time I give a speech about Caterina's Club, I feel as if I'm not alone on the stage. Every single child who has grown by eating the pasta, the families who have created safe and secure homes for themselves, the teens who are building their future—they are all there with me. Being their voice is the greatest gift.

It meant the world to me when Pope Francis recognized our work and I received the following note from Monsignor Konrad Krajewski, Archbishop of Beneventum and Almoner for His Holiness Pope Francis:

> "Dear Bruno, I have the pleasure to send you the crown of the rosary on behalf of the Holy Pope Francis. He will remember you during his prayers and sends you a big brotherly hug from his heart and the apostolic blessing to you and all the people who are helping through gifts of pasta for the hungry. I am also sending you my personal prayers."

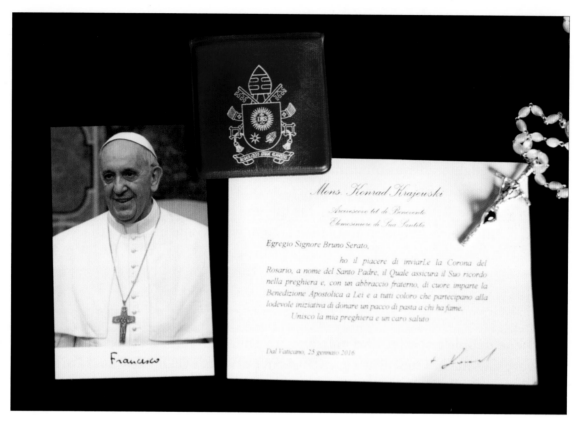

The crown of the rosary that Chef Bruno received from Pope Francis

One of the most illustrious individuals I've come in contact with as a result of my dedication to Caterina's Club is the Dalai Lama. On the occasion of his eightieth birthday, he told me with his beautiful words that a person learns compassion from their mother, and his words meant the world to me. What an experience it was to be touched by his enlightenment.

I always talk about how we need to stop talking about problems and start doing something about them. Words, however, are important because they can draw our attention to a subject and they can also help us make sense out of an event after it has occurred. But in between, there needs to be action. Pasta can be that action, and its power is undeniable.

IX

ITALY: THE LAND OF LOVE AND GENEROSITY

"Being willing is not enough; we must do."
—LEONARDO DA VINCI

Weddings are special, particularly when they take place in Italy and involve a big family. It had been thirteen years since the last wedding in the Serato family. So when we heard the news, we were all overjoyed. My nephew Mattia was getting married, and we were especially happy that his mother, my sister Flavia, would be among us to celebrate with the young couple. Ten years earlier, we nearly lost her when she suffered an aneurysm.

It was noon, and I was working in the restaurant when my brother Freddy had called to tell me our sister was at the hospital with a brain hemorrhage. A friend of mine had died the same way several years ago, and I couldn't get that memory out of my head. By three in the afternoon I was on a plane to Italy, and as soon as I landed in Verona, I rushed to the hospital. I remained there for the next three weeks, massaging her feet and, with Stella's help, doing my best to comfort her. Miraculously, Flavia survived.

So, when she called to let me know about the wedding, I was thrilled.

"My eighteen-month baby is getting married!" she laughed, recalling the events surrounding Mattia's birth, almost a tradition in the family whenever a milestone occurred in his life.

Flavia and her husband already had two daughters when she became pregnant for the third time. They were hoping for a boy, and the baby took his time, arriving well past the official due date. I wouldn't miss Mattia's wedding for the world, I told her, and with that first piece of what would become a tight-fitting puzzle, I began to plan the rest of my trip to Italy. Every time I travel somewhere, I seek out opportunities to spread the word about Caterina's Club, and this time was no different.

Stella and I arrived in Italy three weeks before the big day, and the excitement was already at a fever pitch. But thoughts of the wedding didn't distract Mattia and me from teasing each other. We share a love of soccer, but we root for rival teams: He is a Milan fan, and I am a Juventus supporter. In fact, my team had just won the Italian championship ten days or so before I arrived, and of course I had to remind him of the fact!

In the early years when I returned to visit my family, I was often struck by what seemed to be the grimness of it all. The streets were narrow and dingy, the houses looked old, the people seemed to lack good manners. Yet, with time, I came to realize that those were images created by my own mind so that I would not suffer for my decision to settle in Orange County. Like white blood cells that course through your blood when there's an infection, the negative impressions fought to protect me from an illness known as homesickness.

I've grown up since then and have no doubts that the life I have created for myself in America suits me perfectly. That's not to say the distance from my family has not been hard, especially as Mamma's health began to fail. But now when I return to Italy, I can appreciate its beauty. I am charmed by the old buildings and squares, I soak up the generosity and warmth of friends and strangers alike, and I revel in the burst of flavor I find in every dish, in every glass of wine. I feel at home but also see the land of my youth as if from afar.

Of course, as soon as Stella and I arrived, we all got together to share a meal—brothers, sisters, husbands, wives, sons, and daughters. Ironically, we spend more time together now than we did before, and I'm also able to do more work for the good of Caterina's Club.

I had a busy itinerary planned for my trip and an important job to do: Get the word out about Caterina's Club in order to garner further support from Italian businesses and organizations. Italians are notoriously generous, especially when they can see with their own eyes or touch with their own hands the recipients of their donations. We seek direct contact with others and thrive on the joy it gives us.

The first stop on my Italian trip was the Casa Sebastiano for autistic youth in Trento, where young people afflicted with autism will be able to find a supportive, family-like atmosphere and opportunities for growth. The house was scheduled for grand opening at the end of 2016. The overseeing association, Fondazione Trentina per l'Autismo, and Caterina's Club are now sister organizations through a promise for reciprocal support. I know that there are more and more children born with autism every year, and my hope is to create a link between Trento and California to help children and families. I am dedicated, through Caterina's Club, to helping in any way possible to make their lives better.

When I started planning my time in Italy, Casa Sebastiano was high on my list. I had heard of how the people of Trento, a midsize city in the northern region of Trentino-Alto Adige, had gone from simply talking about something to actually taking action, and I was amazed by their progress. Two outstanding area figures, Giovanni Coletti and Franco Pinamonti, gave me a tour of the large complex set in a beautiful forest.

"In Trentino," explained the president of the regional council, "we seem to have a social conscience in our DNA and are driven to make sure no one is left behind, and we know that we can create a community by sharing food, and that creating a community is a gesture of solidarity."

On the same day I also spent thirteen hours giving interviews and speeches. *Mamma mia!* It was grueling but, honestly, I never tire of speaking about Caterina's Club. My public relations coordinators, Gabrielle Manservisi and Luciano Ferrone, had arranged the interviews back-to-back as a way to maximize my limited time in Italy and the hours quickly became a blur of journalists and events. However, now I look back on the day and recall the mounting enthusiasm surrounding Caterina's Club. A satisfied smile would have lit Mamma's face if she'd been there, each encounter adding momentum to the cause, like yeast added to flour and water. The dough starts out as a small lump, but set in a warm place it begins to rise, getting bigger and bigger. Publicity is an essential element of any endeavor that aims to involve the greater community: You can have the best restaurant, the best-intentioned charity, the most efficiently run organization, but if people are not aware of what you do and how well you're doing it, its growth will surely flounder.

By the end of the day I was so tired I could hardly walk, but I was happy. I felt Mamma was there to silently kiss my forehead when I climbed into bed.

"You've done well, Bruno," she would have said, patting my cheek.

One of the ways I like to relax while I'm in Italy is to wine and dine with family and friends in Soave, which is just outside of Verona. Its medieval castle, perched on a hill and visible for miles, is magnificent, and the white wine is—in my opinion—among the best in the world. In fact, the geography of Veneto makes the area ideal for growing grapes and the wines of the region rank as some of Italy's best—Valpolicella, Amarone, Soave, just to name a few. I *had* to squeeze a day of wine tasting into my schedule!

It was the first of June and spring was giving way to early summer. Yellow, white, and pink wildflowers stood silently under the vines in full bloom, their nearly invisible light green blossoms blending in with the new foliage. I worked my way from one winery to another, reconnecting with my wine-

The beautiful 10th century Soave Castle and Rocca Sveva winery

making friends and the land of my family's origins. It was a fabulous day, and in addition to tasting some great wines I ordered cases to be sent to Anaheim White House for our guests. Several of my favorite wineries of the area are Rocca Sveva, Cantina del Castello, Inama, Cantina Anselmi, Pieropan, Coffele, Cantina Tessari, Garbole, and Dal Forno.

The next official stop on my media marathon was at the headquarters of fresh pasta producer Pastificio Rana. The founder, Giovanni Rana, is like a classic Italian grandfather. He's caring and kind and wants to be sure everyone is happy; his bald head shines in the sun. He was born in a town near Verona, and so we share a common regional heritage and love of many of the same foods. We also share a commitment to making certain that people who don't have enough food are not forgotten.

Giovanni started off as a baker, making bread with his brothers and, after a few years and with the help of the local women, he perfected the skill of making tortellini. He appreciated the manual dexterity it took to shape each one by hand, and in 1959 he began delivering his goods astride his flame red Moto Guzzi motorbike. He carried his precious cargo in a large wicker basket mounted on the back of the bike to families and restaurants along the banks of the Adige River and beyond.

A few years later he set up his own company and has since become an icon among Italian food industrialists, spreading the culture of quality food as a way of life. His biggest competitors, he says, are mothers and grandmothers who make their own fresh pasta at home, and the recipes he uses do not include anything he would not feed to his own grandchildren. This approach to food production in Italy is common, whether it's on an industrial level, in a restaurant, or at home: Italians recognize the importance of using quality ingredients and plenty of love.

Giovanni is a great inspiration. He has never forgotten his humble beginnings and is committed to feeding the less fortunate through generous donations of pasta to the Banco Alimentare, a national network of nonprofit organizations in Italy that promotes the distribution of food and redistribution of excess food to people in need. During our meeting, we spoke about the great power of pasta and discussed how we can assist each other in our efforts to help people who are hungry. His dedication to pasta as a nutritious part of a healthy diet, and his conviction that those who are hungry need good food, make him one of my closest Italian partners.

Over the next few days, I again immersed myself in family. Preparations for the wedding were in high gear with last-minute details on my sister's mind night and day. And yet there was always time for a family meal. One day at a cousin's home, another at a sister-in-law's, always every available chair occupied and lots of good conversation and joking. My brothers and sisters give me strength, and when we're sitting around a table enjoying the recipes Mamma taught us to make, despite the loud voices and apparent chaos, I find peace and balance.

Before Mamma lost her ability to speak, she told us, "After I'm gone, you need to always love each other and stay close." And so each time we come together, in addition to our own simple joy, we know we are respecting her wishes.

Another day, another event. This time, a Power of Pasta party in Ferrara. I had met with secondary school students in the town in February 2015, and after that presentation about Caterina's Club and the "virus of good," they proposed collaborating on a Power of Pasta project to collect food donations for needy families. Of course pasta was the main focus but, in the triangle of cities of Ferrara, Bologna, and Modena, rice is a main part of the local cuisine and so the program was extended to include rice in the food drive. In addition, donations of couscous, the North African sister of pasta made of grains of semolina, were welcome as well as a way to integrate immigrant food traditions.

The school where the event was held is located in the medieval half of the historic town in the Emilia Romagna region. It is the city where Lucrezia Borgia lived, where anti-fascists refused to give in to the political tides in the 1930s and '40s, and where catch nets for debris and fresco "Band-Aids" protect many of the centuries-old buildings that were damaged in the 2012 earthquake. The school is housed in a charming old palazzo that has been modernized to create a mix of massive carved wooden beams, remnants of frescoes, elevators, and modern kitchens. It is a hospitality sciences high school and culinary institute, where students study—alongside normal academic subjects like math, history, Italian, and English—subjects that prepare them for careers in hotels or restaurants. This sort of school is a popular option among secondary school students in Italy, and it is one way that our traditions are carried forward.

I was thrilled to be invited back in 2016 to conclude the food drive, as it again reinforced the idea that words are useful when they're followed up by action. I exchanged greetings with some of the students and shared in their enthusiasm as they snapped selfies with Chef Bruno. I actually remembered a number of them from my initial visit, and it was exhilarating to feel their energy and desire to change the world for the better. Also present for the event were students from area schools who participated in a social network-based project to spread "Italian-ness" to young people abroad through Italy's famous foods, such as pasta, pizza, and gelato. There were joyful voices, spontaneous smiles, and the satisfaction that comes with helping others filled the room.

Just ten minutes before the event was to start, my cell phone rang. The caller ID indicated "unknown." For a moment I considered not answering, since I wanted to give my full attention to the students, teachers, and administrators milling about the sunny assembly area where chairs were set up for the event. But then I thought, *it might be something important,* and I answered.

"Good morning. I'm calling from the Vatican." My heart accelerated and a tremor worked its way up from my knees. "An invitation to the Papal audience in Saint Peter's Square for this coming Wednesday has been approved."

I had been waiting, praying for this opportunity for months. For the next fifteen minutes my legs continued to tremble, and I was so overcome by emotion that I could barely form words. It's a good thing other people were scheduled to speak at the event before me!

One of those people was Fabio Lamborghini, nephew of the founder of the luxury sports car manufacturer, Ferruccio Lamborghini. I had met Fabio the year before at the Lamborghini Museum, where he was the director, and we immediately connected. When I heard him recount how he loved listening to his Uncle Ferruccio, how as a young boy he was mesmerized by his uncle's stories of trial and error and dedication to a dream, I knew we shared a bond. I have a similar relationship with my own nieces and nephews, and getting to know Fabio has been a true pleasure—and a reminder of how important it is for all of us, as adults, to act as role models for younger generations. As soon as I told Fabio about Caterina's Club, he offered his full support and is currently our Italian ambassador.

"Helping Caterina's Club is an opportunity to offer happiness and to be happy in the act of giving," he explained to the students.

When it was my turn to speak, I stepped away from the speakers' table. Every chance I have to communicate with young people is a chance to connect, to transmit directly what Mamma taught me about helping others, and a microphone and a podium often act as a barrier. Surrounded by the teens and the sights and sounds of the school, I felt as if I had traveled back in time to when I was student, happily sharing moments with friends and classmates.

I hadn't prepared a speech; in fact, I never do. For me, words written on a page are rarely the same as the words in my heart.

"What I'm trying to do," I told them, "is make sure that all the children of the world have enough food to eat, and make no mistake, there are children who are hungry on every continent."

I thanked them for their commitment and donations. The room was silent. Empathy and hope colored their faces, and they waited for me to continue.

"A good farmer turns his attention first to his own vegetable patch," I said. "He hoes the soil, he waters the plantlets, and shares the harvest with his family and his neighbors. And through his hard work and generosity, he teaches his children to do the same."

I am always touched when young children come to my restaurant, carrying a package or two of pasta for the kids. When I tell them about what we do, they look at me as if I am reciting a beautiful poem, and then often ask, "Is there something else we can do to help you, Bruno?" It melts my heart every time. When you learn through example and practice to help others—for example the generosity of our neighbors who gave hand-me-downs to Mamma for her seven growing children, and Papa's habit of inviting hungry strangers to sit down for a meal with us—it becomes a way of life.

"We see so many ugly things each day on television; isn't it better to see young people—like you—helping others?" I asked the students.

They smiled and nodded. The virus of good strikes again!

"Listen to your mother," I told them. "Mine told me to make a plate of pasta for a few kids, and look what happened!" They laughed.

The day was also special because two of my brothers and their wives, and both of my sisters, came to Ferrara to show their support. After the scheduled events we spent several hours visiting the city, then ducked into a local *osteria* for a bite to eat and to escape the rain and give my poor aching feet a rest! It was a nice surprise to run into a young man, now working at the *osteria*, who had been a student the prior year at the hospitality school. I was reminded of our own Hospitality Academy students in Anaheim and how they are working toward their future. With good training and solid skills, young people have a better chance at finding steady employment and success.

The next several days were intense. I had speeches to give, I needed to complete the procedural details necessary for the Papal audience—for example, I needed a letter from the bishop in Orange County—and, finally, I needed to get to Rome in time. The invitation had come at the last moment thanks to a friend's uncle, who is a priest, but I still had to pass security clearance. Gabrielle was working hard to put together the pieces, and I continued to concentrate on my schedule and pray that it would all work out.

Before my trip to Italy, I had addressed a letter to Pope Francis to request his help in my fight to end hunger. My proposal was to encourage every single church and religious gathering place, of every single religion, in every city, of every country, to collect pasta and sauce or rice during their religious services, to be distributed later to the hungry in their communities. In my eager attempt to gain the Pope's attention, my aim was to meet him in the Vatican. After the phone call I received in Ferrara, I felt one step closer.

My next big event was at the University of Padua on Tuesday to give a speech to the Rotary Club. It is one of the most prestigious and oldest universities in Europe, as it was founded in 1222. When I walked to the front of the famous Galileo Galilei lecture hall at the university, I felt as if I were in someone else's body. I had left school at a young age, and there I was, in the very room where four hundred years before the "father of modern science" taught mechanics to curious students. And I had come to talk about the simplicity of a plate of pasta and the inspiration from my mother, the daughter of humble shepherds. This was another example of the power of pasta: the power to bring people together, to talk about the importance of healthy food and about avoiding waste in one of the cathedrals of higher learning.

Word arrived from the Vatican at 5:00 p.m., just as I was finishing my speech. There was not sufficient time to complete the security clearance, and so my meeting with the Pope would have to take place on my next trip to Italy. The secretary assured Gabriele, who took the call, however, that the invitation would not be forgotten. Obviously it was a disappointment, but I did feel a twinge of relief. I was exhausted from two weeks of nonstop events and, when my chance comes to meet His Holiness, I want to be at the top of my form, not tired from late-night travel. It is best not to rush certain things. God has his own sense of timing.

The day of my nephew's wedding was drawing closer, and I had one more major event on my schedule: the fifth edition of the Pasta World Championship in Parma, sponsored by the Academia Barilla. Parma is a small city located about midway between Milan and Bologna in the great plain of the Po River, and it is the heart of what is known as "The Italian Food Valley." This is the home of Parmigiano Reggiano cheese, Parma ham, and a long list of other delectable food products of excellence, many of which have DOP and IGP recognition for their long-standing quality and link between man and the land. For its contribution to the culture of food, Parma has been recognized by UNESCO as one of the "Creative Cities of Gastronomy" and it is also home to Barilla, the pasta giant.

The international competition brings together highly acclaimed chefs, using pasta in innovative recipes. Originally Barilla had asked me to be one of the judges for the three-day event, but the wedding coincided with the final day.

"My sister will kill me if I don't come to the wedding!" I told them. So, they offered me space to speak during the highly publicized event about the role restaurants can play in fighting hunger.

My hope was that the competing chefs would take the Caterina's Club model back home with them to their own countries. On the day I attended, I witnessed the creativity of young chefs in the Young Talent competition. The competitors were from all over the world and their recipes were fantastic. In the end, the winner was a young Italian woman named Caterina (!), who pre-pared spaghetti with sea aroma and black pasta carpaccio. A highly innovative and beautiful dish.

It was a wonderful day at one of the cathedrals of pasta. Paolo Barilla and I strengthened the ties between his company and Caterina's Club, and we dis-cussed the possibility of creating a special Caterina's pasta! I couldn't be happier.

Finally, it was time to return to San Bonifacio and give my full attention to the family festivities. In addition to all the Seratos, of course Mattia's child-hood friends had been invited, too. These were young people who were like additional children for Flavia. As kids, they often went to her house to eat and now, as young adults, they were leaving the parental nest and making their own way into the world.

Seratos love parties and celebrations—birthdays, graduations, and espe-cially weddings—because it always means that the family gets together. We like to mark special occasions with special attention: It's our way to show how much we love one another. The first step is getting dressed up. Italians like to look good, but you don't have to spend a lot of money to look good. The trick is how you wear it! So on the morning of the wedding, we fixed ourselves up as if we were going to a fashion show, each of us revealing our own unique style. Flavia, as the mother of the groom, was radiant in a long, royal blue dress that highlighted her beautiful face and blond hair.

It was a warm spring day, perfect for a wedding. Guests arrived at the medieval church of San Giorgio amid hugs and kisses and photos. Neighbors and family, people who hadn't seen each other for years, guests introduced to each other for the first time, children dressed in their Sunday-best, well-wishers who stopped by just to share in the celebration—the atmosphere surrounding an Italian wedding is immediately contagious. Shortly before the ceremony was scheduled to begin, the groom arrived behind the wheel of a vintage, baby-blue Fiat 500, that tiny Italian car that was the basic vehicle for millions of Italian families in the 1960s. More hugs, more photos.

Guests filled the simple, ancient stone church, sunlight streaming through the leaded-glass windows, and continued to chatter as they waited for the bride. When Arianna and her father appeared in the open doorway, everyone hushed. She looked splendid in a long, white, embroidered gown with a full-length veil. She was truly beautiful.

The Catholic ceremony followed the traditional rite, and I even returned to my childhood when I helped the priest as an acolyte. The bells rang in celebration when the ceremony was finished, and the newlywed couple took their first steps out of the church into a shower of rice and rose petals. Bottles of spumante were waiting on ice for the first of many toasts.

The second and, some people would say, best part of an Italian wedding is the lunch. Mattia and Arianna opted for the lovely Relais Villa Bella in San Bonifacio, less than a quarter of a mile from where Mamma and Papa were married in 1945.

The ivy-covered villa, set in a lush, green park, was an ideal setting, with plenty of outdoor space for the *aperitivo* and a lovely dining room for the sit-down meal. Of course, as a restaurateur, I'm always curious to note how other restaurants organize their dining room, and I couldn't help but notice as soon as I walked in that the wedding couple's table was set up on one side of the room. After many years as a maître d' and with the staff's permission, I went to work, moving their table to the center. All eyes should be on them and their happiness. Later, I also removed my tie and acted as waiter! I served the wedding couple all night, and they said it was the best service ever. A spirit of joking and fun is often a part of wedding celebrations, and there was no lack of either during the festivities, which continued into the night with music and dancing.

And the food was delicious, highlighting local dishes like polenta with *baccalà*, *risotto*, and *filetto*.

As the airplane taxied the runway the next day, preparing to take off from Milan, I leaned my head back against the seat and closed my eyes, reflecting on the prior three weeks. I had traveled around northern Italy, giving speeches about Caterina's Club, telling the story of how a simple suggestion from Mamma was changing lives. I had brought her love back home. When we started making pasta for the kids in 2005, no one had any idea how far those plates of spaghetti would reach, and I had no specific goal beyond making sure the children in my neighborhood went to bed with warm food in their stomachs.

The plane lifted and banked, and I looked out the window at the countryside below. It had been a good trip, despite it being exhausting. Once again, I'd been blessed with the love of my family and the opportunity to share in the creation of memories. And the heartfelt reception and support I received over and over again from major figures in the Italian food industry and my countrymen filled me like a generous portion of lasagna. I was full and I gave myself to the drowsiness that follows a good meal.

Seven hours later we landed in New York, where I still had one final, important event. The next day I was scheduled to give a speech at the United Nations as part of the Global Entrepreneurship Initiative Forum. The thought of Mamma's name and memory entering into the glass tower where peace and war have been debated for years brought tears to my eyes, and I hadn't even set foot inside yet!

After checking into my hotel in Times Square, I had a few hours free before the pre-event, black-tie reception in the evening. I wandered around the outside of the United Nations building in the warm sunshine, as if in a daze. A breeze lifted the long line of flags, unfurling their collage of colors. As I took a selfie, to prove to myself that I was really there, I listened distractedly to the cocktail of languages of the visitors standing outside. *Somebody pinch me!*

I had been allotted thirty minutes for my speech and planned to focus on the three pivotal projects of Caterina's Club: Feeding the Kids in America, Welcome Home, and Chef Bruno's Hospitality Academy. I spent the night in agitated sleep, reviewing in my mind the speeches I'd given up until then and how this one carried so much more weight.

When I passed through the gate at the UN Headquarters the next morning, my eye was caught by the famous giant bronze sculpture *Sphere Within Sphere* by the Italian artist Arnaldo Pomodoro. I began to really think about where I was and what was awaiting me. I was overwhelmed with emotion in 2011 when I gave a speech on Capitol Hill, and Mamma's name was mentioned as I received the President's Volunteer Service Award, but walking into the United Nations was even more powerful. Imagine how you would feel if your own mother were talked about in such a revered place. *Mamma mia!*

I survived my emotions and my speech went well. I explained that in America we have a problem with hunger, citing the number of people—and children—who are food insecure but also insisting that if I could help reduce that hunger then so could others.

"Last year I celebrated the first million meals served," I said. "It's amazing to know that one restaurant, one chef can do that—obviously with the help of my crew. But imagine if every restaurant in the country followed my step. We can resolve the problem of hunger in the US and around the world."

I concluded my speech, saying, "With the power of pasta, we can feed the world . . . Hand and hand together, we can change the world."

My speech was well received, and when I finally left the UN I was in need of some pasta and a glass of wine. I crossed Manhattan and headed for the Meatpacking District, where I had dinner at the Giovanni Rana Pastificio restaurant. The welcome I received helped melt my nerves and I felt at home. The chef was from Verona, as were many of the waiters, and each pasta dish was more delicious than the one before. *Viva la pasta!*

Finally, it was time to return home to Orange County. After three weeks in Italy with my family, I felt grounded and ready to face whatever God had in store for me. My mission—at least for this trip—was complete and I was satisfied. The following months and years will hold more challenges and, with Mamma walking beside me in spirit, it is with dedication and conviction that I go forward.

X

ALWAYS LISTEN TO YOUR MAMA

"All that I am, or hope to be, I owe to my angel mother."
—ABRAHAM LINCOLN

I had been aware that Mamma's end was approaching and prayed for her every day. In my prayers, I always asked God to spare me that same phone call I received when my father passed away. I asked earnestly that He let me be with her, together with the rest of her children, when she left this earth.

One day in late summer 2014, I noticed in my safe a Mother Teresa medal strung on a line of rosary beads that I'd put away for safekeeping, and I slipped it around my neck so that the medallion was close to my heart. I have always been deeply devoted to Mother Teresa and I needed to feel her protection. I prayed that Mamma would not suffer any more than she already had through her years of Parkinson's.

Four days later, on the 5th of September, my brothers called to let me know she had taken a turn for the worse. I was crushed. I called several times over the following hours to find out how she was doing: Her ninetieth birthday was seventeen days away, and it felt like such an important milestone. We weren't planning a party because of her health problems, but I did have a plane ticket in hand and was looking forward to giving her ninety kisses on her special day. But God had other plans. Late in the afternoon, I was on a Skype call with the family. I asked Mamma's sister, my Aunt Ivana, to go into Mamma's bedroom to tell her I was on the line and that I loved her. A few minutes later she reappeared on the screen and told me Mamma had reacted with a tiny jolt. For the past ten years I had Skyped Mamma every morning and never missed a day. I craved for Mamma to hear me say those words so I asked my brother Freddy to put me on the speaker phone, because Skype was not in her bedroom.

"Mamma, I'm coming home in a few days. Wait for me. You know how much I love you. I'm coming home to give you ninety kisses. I love you so much."

Then I heard everyone begin to sob in the background; she had passed.

Thank you, God, for letting those be the last words she heard . . . and for sparing me the phone call I never wanted to receive. Thank you for letting me be there, along with my brothers and sisters, by her bedside. Even if it was via speaker, I was there.

Then I, too, let my tears flow without restraint. The date of September 5, 2014, was the same day that Mother Teresa had died seventeen years earlier.

I caught the first flight I could back to Italy. As I was walking down the jetway toward the plane, it came to mind that this was the first time Mamma wouldn't be there when I got home. I shamelessly burst into tears. The flight attendant thought I was afraid of flying and tried to reassure me, but the pain I felt was so deeply embedded in my heart I was paralyzed. When people tell you they've lost their mother, you feel badly for them, but when it happens to you, you finally realize what it really means. The pain is indescribable.

All four of my brothers were waiting for me at the airport in Verona. I was engulfed in their hugs and we shared our tears. We had to wait three days for my sister Stella because she had not been able get a flight back home to Italy with me. I spent those three days next to my mother's special casket at home, surrounded by a photo of the Virgin Mary and lots of flowers. It gave me three extra days to be next to her and to see her look so beautiful now that she was no longer suffering and asleep forever. It made me stronger in this difficult moment.

Through her actions, Mamma had taught my siblings and me about love and compassion, and she had given us everything we could ever need. In the days following that final phone call, we not only felt melancholy but also so full of her love.

The church filled with family and friends for her funeral. There wasn't a dry eye. Mamma had touched the lives of so many people. The priest even mentioned that he had never seen his church so full, and I wasn't surprised. I knew Mamma was loved like this. During the service I gave the eulogy. I began by describing what the word *mother* meant to me. It meant birthday, Easter, Christmas, Thanksgiving, smiles, tears, joy, happiness, emotion, selflessness, comfort, compassion, life, and, obviously, pasta!

I also shared what I thought were the three most important questions I had ever asked her. The first was what had been the best day of her life.

"There hasn't been only one, but each day when one of my children was born," she'd told me.

As I said those words, I paused and looked at my brothers and sisters. "Her answer was dedicated to you and to me," I said.

I can't describe how deep the hurt was in that moment. My second question, I explained, was about the worst day of her life.

"It was when my first baby Corrado died," she'd replied without hesitation. I had watched the tears spill from her eyes and slide down her face. "It doesn't matter how many years pass. When a child of yours dies, the pain never fades," she'd said.

And my third question was about death. "Are you scared to die, Mamma?" I had asked her.

"Yes, I am," she had said. To my surprise, she immediately added, "But not because of death itself; I'll be going to God. But I don't want to die because I know how much all of you children will suffer. I know how much you love me."

Mamma's answers were so telling about her goodness, never thinking about herself but only about the feelings of her children and others first. I concluded the eulogy by saying that Mamma was right, her kids were suffering.

Maybe even more than she could have imagined.

Sadly, because of how her Parkinson's disease progressed, in her final years Mamma was largely unaware of what Caterina's Club had achieved. A little more than a year before my U.N. speech, Caterina's Club marked what was, until then, its greatest achievement. March 24, 2015, was a beautifully sunny and joyous day. However, sadly, Mamma's place at the table had been vacant for about six months.

There were television cameras from all over the world displaying children and young people who had enjoyed eating Caterina's Club pasta, some of them for years, and families who came to show their appreciation, and probably a hundred volunteers. Mamma's love was in the rays of sunshine, and I saw her in the smiles of every one of the people who crowded on the lawn of the restaurant. She was everywhere, although I missed her terribly—especially on that extraordinary day.

Celebrating Caterina's Club's one-millionth meal! (photo by Tony Zuppardo)

The kids always get excited when we serve dessert! (photo by Tony Zuppardo)

It was a party. The biggest I'd had for the kids at Anaheim White House Restaurant yet. Despite all the preparations that filled my head, I couldn't stop thinking about April 18, 2005, when I served the first pasta meal. The party today celebrated a huge milestone: the one-millionth meal for hungry children. *Mamma mia!*

Many of the boys and girls wore their best clothes, and their faces were bright and happy. I'd planned a special menu, and the kitchen staff had been working for hours. The aroma from giant pots of simmering sauce embraced every single person who attended. Like when a big family gathers for an important anniversary and, as soon as you are welcomed inside the house, the cooking smells envelop you.

The servers—some of whom were celebrities, such as Academy Award winner Mira Sorvino, and other regular restaurant customers—brought out pasta with Mamma's tomato sauce, with plenty of veggies hidden inside, then beef tenderloin, seared and slow-roasted until it was still juicy but with a crispy crust, and potatoes, fruit, and finally profiteroles for dessert. I stood off to the side and silently watched the children working so hard to use good table manners. I think my heart grew ten sizes bigger on that one day.

I shook hands with a young man who had been eating Caterina's Club pasta for ten years. "Your pasta is *so* good, Bruno."

A girl with a bright pink ribbon in her hair said, "When I'm a mother, Bruno, I'm going to make this pasta for my children."

I saw a boy with the broadest smile on his face I'd ever seen. I could tell he understood the power of pasta.

One million! I felt as if I'd gone to the moon.

Many people don't realize that hunger is an issue in our own neighborhoods. No child in America—or anywhere for that matter—should go hungry. No boy or girl should be so starving that he or she cannot concentrate at school and appreciate the simple joys of childhood. No single child, regardless of whether he or she lives in a motel or an apartment complex or a house, should ever be denied the necessary nourishment that healthy food provides. It's a question of basic human rights.

When children and families are given the chance to be healthy, to create a home in safe surroundings, and to work for decent wages, our communities flourish. When our communities flourish, our societies advance. And an advanced society takes care of the individuals who form it. It is the goal to which we aim.

The thought of one million plates of pasta for the kids was beyond my comprehension back on that day in 2005. If I lined up the strands of spaghetti, how far would they reach? As long as the Great Wall of China? Halfway to the moon? I have to wonder what the next eleven years hold in store, what will be Caterina's Club's next great achievement . . . only my boss, the Big Man Upstairs, knows that. But what I do know is that I will continue to do my best to honor Mamma's long years of caring and devotion, and I will share her love wherever I can. I want Mamma to be proud.

I let my eyes scan the room full of happy people—school-age children wearing brightly colored t-shirts and sneakers, older and younger siblings, mothers, fathers, and grandparents—then I looked up toward heaven. *This is all because of you,* I told Mamma silently. *None of it would have happened without you and your love.*

When we had our tiny trattoria back in Italy, Mamma and I worked every day, side by side, for eighteen hours straight.

"You're a good boy, Bruno. You'll grow to be a good man," she used to say when we locked up at night.

Chef Bruno with Mamma Caterina on her 80th birthday

As I stood in my restaurant, taking in the evidence of all that Caterina's Club had achieved—the faces, the sounds, the aromas, the love—I heard her voice say it again as lovingly as ever. I hoped to God that somehow she was looking down, watching all that we were doing in her name. The first time she held me in her arms and kissed me on the day of my birth—in the morning on the seventh day of October—I looked up at her and discovered unconditional love.

Mamma is the heart of Caterina's Club, and everyone who works to help the kids has a piece of her inside them. Her heart has never really stopped beating. Each person who joins our mission carries her life force, pumping love back to the heart. Mamma Caterina still lives, her love pulsing through us as we do our best to help others and, following her example, to care for children who deserve a healthy start in life. Caterina, a mother of seven children, now a mother of millions. Ciao, Mamma.

Sì, caro.

XI

New Beginnings

"God gives his toughest battles to his strongest soldiers."
—Anonymous

February 3rd

5:00 p.m.—What a bustling night at the restaurant! We are busy preparing for the upcoming Valentine's Day weekend, when all the lovers come in and scatter love all around us. We've been hard at work, ordering more food and creating our "Romeo and Juliette" menu, which features heart-shaped ravioli, filet mignon, and lobster, and a heart-shaped chocolate dessert. It's always an exciting week. Everyone dresses up—the men wear their best Italian suits and walk proudly next to their stunning dates. People want to take their partners out to the most romantic restaurant in the area, and Anaheim White House Restaurant is considered the most romantic in Orange County. It looks so majestic and luminous with its sparkling white lights at night that anyone who walks in after the sun sets will say, "Wow, this place is gorgeous." We are usually sold out that entire week.

After a busy Friday night, I am working late in the office, revising the invitation for our thirtieth anniversary celebration on April 2nd, the same day as my father's birthday. I can't believe that thirty years have passed—it feels like only yesterday that I was struggling to find a way to purchase and renovate the restaurant. So many weeks, months, and years flew by in the blink of an eye that I still can't imagine how I have now been here half of my life. I still love this place that is like home to me and enjoy being here every day. I love my customers, my crew, and every corner of this magnificent, elegant restaurant that has enriched my life and enabled me to help others.

The past thirty years have filled it with meaningful moments and memories. I have witnessed so many of my friends on their first dates, having a first kiss, and even proposing. I've seen people laugh and cry, and my restaurant has often been a part of the most important day in their lives. I have met some of my best friends here—and I can still remember the table where they were sitting thirty years ago. When NHL player Bobby Ryan took his date, Danielle, out for Valentine's Day they sat in the Ronald Reagan room, and now she is his wife. Andrea Bocelli and Gwen Stefani both sat in the Lincoln room. I smile as I think of so many beautiful nights filled with great food, wine, and laughter, that we've had in the past thirty years.

11 p.m.—I am getting tired, so I decide to finish up the invitation the next day and drive home to Huntington Beach. As I drive along the Pacific Coast Highway, I gaze at the ocean and think, *I'm so lucky to be in California next to the water and to have a restaurant this beautiful near Disneyland—the happiest place on earth.* Everything looks as if I am going to enjoy the rest of my life where I want to be.

I take a shower before going to bed and watch the news for thirty minutes to see what happened around the world today. As we all know, the news is often disturbing—terrorist attacks, earthquakes where people have lost their lives, protesters around the world, and so much more. I decide to change the channel to a television show that will relax me and help me fall sleep: *The Golden Girls.* I can't believe that this amazing actress, Betty White, still kicks butt and makes me laugh with her humor, even today. I turn off the TV as my eyes begin to close with exhaustion. Instead of sleeping like an angel, I find myself tossing and turning, maybe because I am overtired.

1:55 a.m.—Saturday, in the early morning, my best friend, Jiri, from Prague voice texts me. He loves to wake me up in the middle of the night to make me laugh. Sometimes I want to kill him, because I can't go back to sleep after his damn game of waking me up with so many text messages. Tonight the joking continues all the way until 4:33 a.m. One of my last texts to him is "people sleep in my country at this early time," and he answers, "I am not in your country and I don't sleep." You can tell from this what a funny guy he can be, and honestly he has made me laugh often for the past seventeen years. With all the work and stress that you experience in life, there is nothing better than a great laugh to make you feel better. I am now ready to go back to sleep after this great laugh. I feel happy that I have a happy life and everything is going well.

4:32 a.m.—During my conversation with Jiri, someone had called me from an unknown number. Obviously I did not answer it in the middle of the night, thinking that it was another phone prank or a wrong number. Soon after I hang up the phone with Jiri, I notice that the person who called has left me a voice message. Hmmm . . . is this the night of joking? I almost don't want to listen to the message right now because I'm so tired, but I know it will bother me until I know who called me. I always like to take care of work—or anything in life— today because tomorrow it's already too late.

4:38 a.m.—I listen to the message, and I think it must be a joke. A man's voice says, "Hello, I am looking for Bruno Serato. I'm sorry, but I have bad news for you. Your restaurant is on fire."

I call him back at 4:39 a.m. and say, "Hello, why are you calling me at 4:30 in the morning? Is it a joke or what?"

The voice at the other end does not sound like someone who is joking. It is somber and repeats the same thing I just heard. "I have very bad news for you, Mr. Serato. Your restaurant is on fire, and a lot of fire trucks are on site already."

I have to ask him again, "Is this a joke or what?"

He says, "No, you should go there ASAP."

My next question, since I am not yet convinced, is, "How did you get my personal cell number?"

He answers, but I only vaguely hear him say something about a fireman, because at this point my adrenaline has kicked in and I'm preoccupied with the fear that my restaurant really is on fire—every restaurateur's worst nightmare. The man on the phone says he works for Bison, a property restoration company, and a joke comes to mind. Bison is one of the leanest meats you can find, and lately I have been eating it a few times a week. "Is that a food joke or what? Are you crazy or what?" I ask. Nothing is making sense, and everything feels oddly surreal.

But after several seconds I begin to feel like it's not a joke; it could be real. My beloved Anaheim White House could be burning down.

"Okay, I'm on my way," I reply and hang up the phone quickly.

I put on some pants and race down the stairs five at a time, get in my car, and drive like I have a Ferrari in the direction of Anaheim. On my way there I call my right-hand man and nephew, the general manager of the restaurant, Sylvano. He does not answer, and I leave him a message to call me immediately. *Will he listen to it before I get to the restaurant? Did Sylvano receive a phone call, too?* His number is the actual emergency contact for the fire department and police department because I travel to Europe so often. His number is the first on the list and mine is the second. I hope that means this is all a sick joke if Sylvano has not received a call. I feel desperate to get to the restaurant, hoping and praying that it will be just as I left it.

4:55 a.m.—Sylvano calls me as I'm driving like a race car driver on the 22 Freeway eastbound. I tell him about the phone call I received at 4:39 a.m. "Sylvano, someone called me to say that the restaurant is on fire."

"Are you joking?" he asks. Sylvano can't believe it either.

He says he will meet me at the restaurant.

4:58 a.m.—I call my best friend, Jiri, in Prague whom I was laughing with on the phone twenty minutes earlier and tell him what is happening. He asks if I'm joking, but when he hears my voice he knows it's bad. He tells me to call him as soon as I know anything and we hang up.

5:15 a.m.—As I get off the freeway and cross Katella to turn right on Anaheim Boulevard, I start to notice dark smog billowing up into the sky. *Oh my God, is that my restaurant? God, please, no.*

Firefighters working hard to extinguish the fire

I almost blow through two traffic lights before I arrive at the restaurant. The police have closed the street, and I see millions of red lights from all of the fire trucks. It looks like something that I usually see on TV during the news. Since I can't drive all the way to the restaurant because of the street closure, I park as close as possible and run as fast as I can in the middle of the street to get there, thinking *maybe I can try to save it. . . .*

The first person who sees me is the Anaheim fire chief, Randy Bruegman, who knows me very well and who I consider a friend. He approaches me with a sad look on his face, and he hugs me and says, "I am sorry, Bruno, I am sorry."

In that moment I know it is very bad. It takes zero money to be good—and that hug from him was worth a million dollars.

5:20 a.m.—I call my sister Stella to tell her the bad news, but she can't understand what I'm saying—not because of my poor English—but because I'm crying so much that I'm incoherent as I try to tell her that I lost everything and the restaurant is gone.

At first, Stella thinks that someone in the family has died like that day when I called to let her know that Mom had gone to heaven. My tears and crying are uncontrollable, making it harder to explain to people what is happening. As soon as Stella understands, she's on her way to be by my side. In the meantime, Sylvano and his wife, Katie, arrive and all of our tears together are like Niagara Falls.

5:25 a.m.—I have to call my family in Italy; I want them to hear it from me—not from social media or the news. I decide to call my brother Eddie first. He also thinks that someone has died. I am crying so loudly that he can feel my pain and it's like another Niagara Falls in Italy. Soon after, all my brothers and sisters, and family in Italy call and share their profound tears with me. In the best times and worst times, my family is always there. It was something Caterina taught us, and it was the best gift she gave us and the one I love the most.

5:45 a.m.—The firemen are still trying to extinguish the flames. It looks like there are thousands of them, and the first thought that comes to my mind is

Statues amid the rubble of Anaheim White House after the fire (photo by Thierry Brouard / Prémium Paris)

9/11—a tragedy that reminds us of how firemen and police officers came to our aid when we needed help. My tragedy is not even close to that, obviously, but the feeling of losing everything as it goes up in flames is so hurtful that my soul cries out, and it seems as if my heart will stop beating.

5:50 a.m.—As the initial shock wears off, I suddenly realize that one of my workers could have been inside.

"Is anyone hurt? Was anyone inside? Has anyone died?" I ask in a panic.

"No," the chief tells me, and I begin to feel relieved.

I am grieving the loss of my restaurant, but thank God I do not have to grieve the loss of human life.

6:00 a.m.—I still have hope that the fire has damaged only part of the restaurant, but it's too soon to really know. At one point I look up at four firemen on top of the roof and I feel so much respect for them, thinking, *these guys do an amazing job.* A giant flame emerges from where my office is located in the attic, and I'm terrified that one of these men could get hurt because of my restaurant—the restaurant that has given pleasure and love to millions of people since the day that it was built in 1909. Watching the fire on the roof, I realize just how bad this is, and the tears continue to flow as my family hugs me and I stand there devastated.

6:30 a.m.—I'm flooded with phone calls, but I only answer the ones from family. I can't bring myself to talk to anyone else. Not yet.

7:30 a.m.—*What am I going to do about the kids? The pasta? What I am going to do?* Monday we have the kids to feed, and they can't go to bed hungry. I start to worry about it so much, and I can't bear to stop doing what I have been doing for twelve years—serving Chef Bruno's pasta to children in need.

At this point in the morning, I start to answer a few calls to be polite, because I know people are worried. My friends, the event center chef, restaurateurs, and even business competitors begin to contact me, feeling so bad about what has just happened and offering their help. At that moment I realize that the word "competitor" means nothing. When people get together hand in hand to help each other, nothing matters but kindness and love; competition no longer exists.

I hear someone ask, "Do you need a kitchen?" At that moment, I think, *AMEN.*

"A kitchen? Yes! Yes, I do need one."

I don't need a kitchen for me or my customers but for feeding the kids—for the power of pasta. John Machiaverna, the executive director of the Boys and Girls Club of Anaheim, is one of the first friends to arrive that day.

"Bruno, I made five phone calls, and I got kitchens for you to cook the pasta," he says.

I feel so blessed. Here I am in the middle of a tragedy, and I have been blessed with a kitchen for the kids. No words can describe how I feel in that moment . . . hope is already here.

Just a few weeks before we had received a heavenly message to move our office for Caterina's Club to a new location. We worked in the attic for so many years to save money for the foundation, but as our mission grew, it began to feel a bit tight. On January 1st we moved into a new office in downtown Anaheim to be more efficient and have more space. After operating from the restaurant for twelve years, we finally had our own new office. Four weeks later . . . FIRE.

I keep saying that Mamma Caterina sent us a message from heaven to move our mission to feed the children to a new location. She did not want to see the kids suffer. *Grazie*, Mamma Caterina.

7:44 a.m.—I receive a call from one of the hosts at KFI radio 640.

"Bruno! This is Bill Handel. I want to make sure you're okay. I don't want you to worry. Here at the radio the entire crew is behind you 100 percent. We're going to help you. We're going to go through this together. We are behind you until you reopen and after."

Bill and KFI radio have done so much already, and they call me to say they want to do more for me? I have no words. I just feel so blessed again. I am so grateful to Bill and KFI 640.

8:00 a.m.—Some of my friends and crew start to arrive, and tears cascade down each face every time we hug each other. Father Michael is one of them. I ask him if we can hold hands and have him recite a special prayer.

Looking at my crew in tears is absolutely heartbreaking. It hurts me so much to see them in pain, too. Some of the guys who used to work for me start to show up as well, and even some of the people who got fired call to tell me that they feel the pain. It is such an outpouring of love from all of them.

Suddenly, I think of how this is all going to affect my crew. They have families to support, rent, and car payments. How are they going to deal with it now that they have no jobs?

I look at them and say, "I'm going to do everything I can to find you guys jobs." I do not want them to worry that it's over. "I'm still your boss but a boss who cares—now it's my turn to work for you," I say.

8:30 a.m.—I receive more phone calls, but I can only answer the ones with names I recognize. I don't mean to be rude, but it's too much. I am crying too hard to talk. So many people call and ask how they can help.

"Hello, it's Michael, the president of Disneyland Park. How can I help you, Bruno?"

"Hello, it's John, the general manager of the Marriott Hotel. How can I help you, Bruno?"

"Hi, it's Jay, the president of Visit Anaheim. How can I help you, Bruno?"

Jay arrives that morning to hug me; he couldn't bear go to work without showing me his face and giving me a hug.

My first focus after the family and the fire is the pasta for the children, and I was thankfully able to take care of it. The second important focus is my crew. I need to help them. A major company calls, and I ask if they can help me find jobs for my crew or if they can hire them. So many people offer them jobs and I am so thankful. Many of my crew are already taken care of within twelve hours' time.

I ask my crew manager to continue to work for us until the end of March. I want him to take phone calls and to find jobs for every single person in my crew. I could not sleep if I knew there was someone out there suffering. Restaurateurs, chefs, and hotel managers keep calling me to ask if they can hire my people to help. I am so grateful, and I thank God.

9:00 a.m.—I receive a phone call from Luca at Barilla headquarters.

"Hi, Bruno, this is Barilla; how can we help you?" he asks.

The call transports me back to six years ago, when I was running out of pasta and Barilla was the first company to call and ask me if they could donate pasta and tomato sauce. I will always remember that moment. I was so surprised that Barilla was calling me from Italy. I did not know anyone at Barilla back then, and here they are again ready to help.

I don't have enough words of gratitude for all of the people who are calling to offer assistance. My answer is always the same: The kids are taken care of, and I am working on helping out my crew. And me? I don't care about me right now—it's not my priority. I will be the last one on the ship like the captain of the Titanic.

9:30 a.m.—Leslie, Cinzia, David, Tim, Bob, and other close friends walk in, panicked and sad when they see the restaurant, adding more tears. My Australian family, Italian family, Canadian friends, and French friends all express their love and support. It feels like the world is calling me.

10:00 a.m.—Word has spread that a historical landmark is on fire. Reporters arrive to cover the news that Chef Bruno's restaurant had a horrible fire this morning that destroyed it.

11:30 a.m.—The firemen had worked so hard all night that I shake hands with every single one of them and say thank you. They look at me sadly, because even though fighting fires is their job, I know they feel the pain of the people who have worked hard all their lives to see it all destroyed. They are truly amazing.

1:00 p.m.—I finally hear the question I've been waiting for since 4:00 a.m.

"Bruno, would you like to walk in now to see the damage?"

Safety is an issue, and I have to be careful. We can't stay long because the smoke is still in the building, and the fireman, Deputy Chief Tim O'Hara escorts me around the rubble to make sure I am safe. I could not enter the restaurant until they were 100 percent sure it was safe to enter.

1:15 p.m.—I slowly walk in from the back door, where it still looks decent besides the black wall and horrible odor of burning. The first door on my right was once the kitchen door where huge pots of sauce and amazing food were served to presidents and celebrities as well as my many loyal customers and friends—and the children. The kitchen looks untouched. How? This is where the fire must have started, and I'm wondering how this can be possible. . . .

I walk in ten feet more and see the front desk on my left, the spot where I usually stand to hug and kiss customers after I welcome them to my home.

The restaurant computer—where thousands of people have reservations set for the upcoming conventions and Valentine's weekend—sits atop the desk.

I turn my head to the right, where the portrait of the most beautiful woman in the world used to hang on the wall. Mamma Caterina watched over me at work, and her gorgeous eyes never took a break, following me everywhere. The painting had been done on canvas, and I had given a copy to Mamma Caterina for her eightieth birthday and also kept a copy at my house. I needed to see her wherever I went—to work or back home in Italy or at my sister's house or even on the Caterina logo on my business cards. She has never left me.

I break down in tears again. She is not here today to look at me. She probably did not want to see my face as I walked in for the first time after the fire; she knew how much her son would be hurting.

The firemen are still inside, working around the debris, and they ask if there's anything important to me that I want them to try to find. My most prized possession was Mamma's portrait, and it is now gone, but the one other meaningful object that I would love to save is a gift I received from Pope Francis—my rosary. All of my awards over the past years are gone. They were next to the note and rosary from the Pope, so I fear that it will be impossible to find, but I mention it anyway.

The fireman beside me says, "Let's look for it."

The firemen start to dig in the middle of the floor for what feels like hours but is only fifteen minutes. Finally, I have to tell them to please stop looking for it.

"You guys must be exhausted. Don't worry," I say.

I will ask Pope Francis to send me another one if I have a chance. They do not stop looking, and suddenly a voice next to me shouts, "Here it is!" It is my niece Caterina, the first granddaughter of Mamma Caterina, named after her Nonna, who notices the rosary lying on the floor. The rosary is completely black, and part of it is damaged, but the cross of Jesus is still intact and shining. I cannot believe it is the only thing I want and it has been found. I thank Caterina and the firemen and hold the cross in my hand.

"He did not abandon me," I say in a soft voice as I look at the crucifix. "You suffered so much for the world and humanity, so much more than what I suffer today. My suffering is nothing compared to yours."

Faith can give you strength when you need it the most, no matter what religion you practice. This is my religion, and it fills me with renewed strength and hope.

As I look to my left, my eyes rest on the CNN Heroes Award. It has been burned and is a dirty black from the fire and smoke, but it is still there. In that moment, I think all of the firemen are the true heroes, not me. But the award was given to me by Jerry Seinfeld during that event, and I'm thankful that it has not been completely destroyed and lost in the fire. Am I still a hero for a lot of people around the world? Maybe. Even if I am not a hero like so many others, I will try to be one for those who look to me for inspiration. I just need one or two days at least to get over the shock of what has happened.

As I walk through the dining room, I am horrified. For a moment I think it must be Halloween, but the haunted house at Disneyland looks so much more beautiful than this one. It is so awful. That gorgeous room, where millions of customers ate gourmet food, drank incredible wine, flirted, and enjoyed the moment at their table with happiness and love, is suddenly all gone. It doesn't feel real.

I remember how I always shook hands with my customers and asked every table how they were enjoying their dinner. I always walked proudly through my dining room because I knew I had something special. The service, the food, the ambiance, and the presentation were all something classic that never died. Trends come and go but what is classic always remains. Now the dining room looks like a burnt fondue bourguignon. Everything has melted down.

I head upstairs to the third floor all the way to the office and it looks like a horror movie. But it was not a movie—it was real.

I remember the first time that Mamma Caterina was doing a little dancing and singing in the restaurant. I had told her that everything I owned was hers, too. She was proud of me always.

Inside the wreckage of what used to be the dining room (photo by Thierry / Prémium Paris)

I blink back the tears, thinking of this moment. So many things are gone. Thirty years of my life are gone . . . but I still stand.

I cannot take anymore, so I walk out and join my family and friends outside the kitchen back door, who are all looking at me, waiting to see if I say maybe it's not that bad. I look at everyone and cry. It's all gone, but I have my rosary, and I smile a little.

The interior destruction of Anaheim White House Restaurant (photo by Thierry / Prémium Paris)

Holding my precious rosary from Pope Francis—
the beads have been singed but the crucifix remains

3:57 p.m.—The phone rings again, and I know the number so I answer it.

"Hi, Bruno, this is Carlo. I just found out what happened, and I'm shocked and so sad. I am so hurt. I can't believe what happened to you." My friend Carlo Ponti knows what I do so well, because he does something special for kids who love music.

Maestro Carlo Ponti is known for taking audiences of all ages on musical journeys. He has been associate conductor of the Russian National Orchestra since 2000, and in 2013 he founded the Los Angeles Virtuosi Orchestra—an ensemble that emphasizes music's educational value. The Los Angeles Virtuosi Orchestra envisions a world in which every young person has access to music education. The Los Angeles Virtuosi Orchestra has created a new paradigm of giving, allocating 100 percent of net revenue from subscription performances to advance music education. We became friends the very first day we met because we both love to help kids.

After chatting a few minutes, Carlo says, "Hold on one second, Bruno, my mom wants to talk to you."

"Hello, Bruno," echoes a familiar voice. "I am sorry for this bad news. My son Carlo is hurting and feels like someone has passed. He respects you so much and can't believe what happened to you. I want to give you a big hug." It is the beautiful Sophia Loren.

I reply, "I once heard your story that you had to run for shelter with your mom during World War II because of bombing. My situation is not as bad. You represent Italy to me—it's as if you are the statue of liberty of Italy, and I feel like the entire country of Italy has just called me. Not only are you one of the most beautiful women in the world, but you are one of the most beautiful people inside. Thank you, Sophia."

Bruno with Sophia Loren

Sophia Loren's call gives me strength and love. For me that call was not just from Sophia Loren but also from a mamma. *Grazie*, Sophia.

4:25 p.m.—Bobbie Stovall and her grandchild, my youngest guest chef at the restaurant, arrive to check on me. They are in shock. Bobbie and James Stovall have always been there for me; they sold the restaurant to me years ago and have been big supporters of everything I do. And yet again here they are supporting me in my time of need. I thank them.

5:30 p.m.—My brother Eddie, his wife, Ornella, and his niece, Ariana, call from Italy to let me know that they are on their way to America to stay with me and to offer their emotional support on behalf of all the Italian family—in times of sadness or joy, my family is always there for me. The first time I walked into the restaurant, as a guest of the manager, they were with me. They had been here on vacation when I was invited, so I brought them to this place that suddenly had such a profound effect on me, leaving me with a strong desire to own it someday. It will be a much different situation this time.

As the sun sets it brings more darkness on one of my darkest days. I am utterly exhausted, so I decide finally to return home. It feels strange to leave my restaurant alone and unsecured, without defense, but there is nothing to steal—only ashes remain. Just yesterday Anaheim White House Restaurant stood majestically with beauty all around. So much can change in a matter of hours.

10:00 p.m.—I lie in bed, alone for the first time all day. After I close my eyes, I only sleep ten minutes, and as soon I open them I think, *it was just a nightmare; it can't be true. Was I dreaming?*

No, I was not.

The day after the fire is a crazy day, and I am bombarded by television reporters from every corner of the country. Every major television station and newspaper reporter wants to interview me. I want to escape to Italy to stay with my family and run away from everything, but I know I can't. I respect all of them, and they have been so supportive of what we do for the kids. Plus, I also need to tell the country about what happened. I had so many reservations that I need to notify everyone that we had a fire and are closed until further notice. I am grateful to the media for being so helpful to me. *Grazie.*

I am concerned about every single reservation, especially because Valentine's Day is around the corner, and I do not want to disappoint my customers. In fact, that is my other priority right now—to have my hostess on payroll call all the reservations that we had booked for 2017 and let them all know. We had charity events booked, weddings, and lots of corporate meetings. What a mess.

Will it end?

On Monday the television reporters are still here, but for good news this time. After only forty-eight hours of this horrible situation, I am on my way to an event center in Anaheim called Highway 39. My friend Mike is allowing me to use his facility to cook pasta and serve the kids. Woo hoo! I am back to work already, feeding the children. Steve Hartman of CBS News has flown all the way from New York to report on and film the story.

The pasta is on the stove cooking Mamma Caterina style, and I am smiling. I am chopping the carrots, tomatoes, and onions, and my three kitchen crew are here with me. I am feeling much better. Focusing on the kids enables me to forget my own tragedy for a few hours.

The kids from the Anaheim Boys and Girls Club start arriving. I wait by the door for them like it is my first day at school, nervous but exited. The first bus drops off the kids, and one by one they come in. I am not just smiling; I am happy. After the deep sadness of the last two days it seems like a miracle to be able to feel joy again. Feeding the kids pasta and interacting with them is the best therapy for me right now. These kids are my medicine. I love it.

Some kids know what has happened and start to ask me questions or offer a kind word of encouragement.

"Chef Bruno, how do you feel?"

"Chef Bruno, does it hurt to have lost the restaurant?"

"Chef Bruno, I love your pasta."

"Chef Bruno, you cook the best pasta."

I try to hold in my tears because I do not want the kids to get hurt by seeing me so upset. I feel like I have already hurt so many people unintentionally, because they felt pained to see me in such pain. A little six-year-old redhead named John keeps looking at me with sadness on his face, but when he smiles, he helps me to smile in return. That is really the best remedy for a broken heart.

After a couple of hours, the kids get back on the bus, and I am left to clean the kitchen with my crew and with a whole lot of hope. I know things will be better eventually.

The next day I am back to the same routine: the television reporters and the kids. Without the kids, I know it would have been more difficult to survive the first three days, and I am grateful to them. They give me so much more in two days than what I have done for them in twelve years.

At night, after returning home, I spend hours on the computer, thanking the millions of people around the world who texted and e-mailed. I don't take it for granted, and I also leave messages to apologize to those who I have missed and to thank them. I am overwhelmed by the outpouring of love from so many people, many of whom I don't even know.

The facility that has opened its doors for us to cook pasta for the kids is a blessing in the meantime, but I am in search of a more spacious, more efficient kitchen for Caterina's Club. I had planned to start the Chef Bruno Hospitality Program on February 25th, when I would be bringing fifty kids to the restaurant to teach them how to cook, and I will need a larger space.

The Marconi Museum, the Richard Nixon Library, and the Casa Romantica also offer their venues to help, but I want to have a venue that's not far from the restaurant. I receive a call from the Christ Cathedral, and they offer me their own kitchen and rooms indefinitely for my mission. Thank god. The facility is so much bigger and easy to work in that it will make it easier to focus.

I thank all the other venues who have helped us tremendously, but this is where we are going to make our new home.

Once an evangelical megachurch known as the Crystal Cathedral, this landmark building and its thirty-four-acre complex was purchased by the Catholic Diocese of Orange in 2012. It is now a new spiritual center for the more than 1.3 million Roman Catholics in Orange County. Made entirely of glass and surrounded by a beautiful arboretum, this enormous space is truly a gift from God for Caterina's Club and the Chef Bruno Hospitality Program.

Chef Bruno standing in front of Christ Cathedral (photo by Lyle Okihara)

Chef Bruno with trays of pasta, getting ready to serve the children
in his new space (photo by Lyle Okihara)

The kids are all set. The crew is under control. Now what? Oh, yes, I have to take care of my restaurant.

Four days after the fire we receive the report from the investigation that an electric problem sparked the fire at Anaheim White House Restaurant. The authorities confirm that it was accidental. How are we going to deal with the insurance and all the logistics to take care of this situation?

Sylvano and his wife, Katie, have been my right hand, taking care of the insurance and all the details about this nightmare and what we need to think about to move forward. I have had other priorities. I sit down to have a conversation with Sylvano and ask him to give me the good news and the bad news. The bad news? The restaurant is destroyed—80 percent of it is gone. We lost the entire interior, every detail that I created with my heart and soul for thirty years.

The good news? We have insurance with Lloyd's of London. I have been concerned about our coverage, but I know it's a good company, so I feel hopeful. How long will it take? We don't know. This insurance company has been known to take longer than average to pay the coverage, but I have never dealt with them and I can't confirm if that's true. My major concern is that we need to finish the payroll for vendors and others.

Our insurance agent, William Germani, is incredibly helpful. I find out that when you have a fire you need to take action to put the property in safety mode or you could get in trouble with your own insurance. We hire Bison Property Restoration company for the night of the fire, and they close down the property until further notice. I now understand why the man who called to notify me about the fire mentioned "Bison."

Many people text me and call me to give me their opinion on how to handle everything. Do this. Don't do this. Do that. Don't do that. It is so confusing that they make me nervous and insecure about what decision to make. The major issue at this point is whether or not I should hire a public adjuster to deal with the insurance and everything else. Obviously, you have to pay them and it can burn through your insurance settlement—and that's assuming you receive all of your expected coverage. At this point I have no idea if we will or not, but it would be nice to hire an expert who knows how to handle these situations. Sylvano, Katie, and I talk every hour on the hour to make the decision. Yes or no? I ask Sylvano to give me twelve hours to decide.

The next morning, I call Sylvano and tell him to hire the public adjuster to give us a break. I select a company named Greenspan and they take over dealing with all the insurance logistics. Now we can finally breathe a little.

The city of Anaheim has been my home for thirty years and has always been supportive of my restaurant and charity. On the morning of the fire, the mayor, Tom Tait, City Councilmen Steve Fessel and Kris Murray, and so many other officials stopped in to see me and hug me. They were all sad to see this gorgeous building almost completely destroyed, and they know me so well that they feel my pain, too. They offered me 100 percent assistance from the city for all my needs to rebuild it as fast is possible, and, in fact, in five days the entire city of Anaheim has been there to help. They even assigned a task force to expedite any problems. I am so thankful to the city of Anaheim and all of the various people who have come forward to offer their extraordinary generosity and support.

My longtime friend and publicist, Frank Groff, created a gofundme page on the day of the fire to help raise money to rebuild the restaurant and provide financial relief for my employees. More than 1,800 people raised more than $167,000 in just three weeks. It will cost at least a million dollars to rebuild Anaheim White House Restaurant, but this is only the beginning of fundraising efforts. I have been completely overwhelmed by such an outpouring of love and donations. I wish I could thank each and every person. Please know that your support means the world to me. One woman gave $5 and apologized for not being able to afford to give more and I was so touched. You need zero money to be a good person, and that $5 was worth a million to me. . . .

Some chefs and the restaurateur of Highway 39 also planned an event to raise money for my crew and for Caterina's Club. I was yet again overwhelmed by the love that people expressed for me and my crew. Money poured in to help my waiters, waitresses, busboys, and kitchen crew pay their rent and support their families. It was the first night that I was reunited with my second family— my Anaheim White House Restaurant crew—and I will never forget the emotion I felt having us all together again.

Greg Gorman, celebrity photographer, has donated a photo session to raise money for the restaurant, with bids starting at $5,000. He has generously included prints, as well as hair and makeup. And the dear Anaheim Ducks hockey team gifted me with a #87 jersey, the year I opened the restaurant, signed by all the players. So many people have offered help or a kind word.

Feeding the children through Caterina's Club has been a passion for me, because I simply can't bear the thought of a child going hungry. When I was struggling to make ends meet, I didn't really think about it—I just did what I had to do to make sure those kids got a hot meal. But the experience of the fire has shown me that when you care about your community, your community cares back. I may have lost my restaurant, but I didn't lose the love of those around me. It is humbling and beautiful to feel so much love.

What's next? Thirty years later, after buying the restaurant, here I stand, thinking about my future. Thirty-five years ago I left my country to start a new future in a country where my dream came true. Will I start again in the same country to see if my dream can still come true again? Is this ending really a new beginning?

Recipes

APPETIZERS/SMALL PLATES

ENTREES

DESSERTS

APPETIZERS/
SMALL PLATES

AHI TARTARE Serves 4

Popularity of raw fish in the United States is mainly from an Asian influence and is something I personally love. I created my tartare dish to include a simple Italian touch by adding flash fried pasta "sticks." I love the way it makes the recipe both crunchy and soft in texture. The chili vinaigrette is what gives the ahi tartare a touch of magic.

AHI:

¾ pound sushi-grade ahi tuna (chopped)

Splash of lemon juice

Splash of caper juice

1 teaspoon extra-virgin olive oil

Sprinkle of parsley

Salt and pepper to taste

2 tablespoons chili vinaigrette (see recipe below)

CHILI VINAIGRETTE:

½ cup extra-virgin olive oil

2 roasted red bell peppers, minced

½ medium red onion, minced

½ tablespoon chili flakes

1 tablespoon chili powder

Salt and pepper to taste

AVOCADO MOUSSE:

½ avocado

1 teaspoon lemon juice

Salt and pepper to taste

½ cup salmon pearls/salmon caviar

1 (3-inch) ring cookie cutter

1. Combine all ahi ingredients in a large bowl.

2. In a separate bowl, mix all ingredients for the chili vinaigrette.

3. Slowly add small amounts of the 2 tablespoons of the chili vinaigrette to the ahi mixture until the desired consistency is reached, and save any leftover vinaigrette for another purpose.

4. Remove avocado from skin and place into a small bowl. Mash the avocado with a fork, then add lemon, salt, and pepper, and stir together until a mousse-like texture is formed.

5. Using the cookie cutter ring as a mold, place the ahi mixture inside. Spread a layer of avocado mousse over completed mixture, remove cookie cutter, and finally garnish with salmon caviar.

photo by Lyle Okihara

DUCK LEGS IN POTATO NESTS Serves 6

I grew up seeing ducks in my backyard the first ten years I lived in France. As we all know, Duck à l'Orange is one of the most famous French dishes. We raised ducks (and rabbits) for the purpose of eating them, and they were often on the menu at Trattoria Cristallo, our family restaurant in Italy. On special Sunday occasions and holidays Mamma Caterina would prepare duck. This baked duck recipe is my twist on her famous duck dish.

DUCK:

Pinch of fresh garlic, minced
Pinch of fresh rosemary, minced
Salt and pepper to taste
6 duck legs
2 ounces (¼ cup) micro greens
¼ cup + 2 tablespoons grenadine
   liqueur

SAUCE:

½ shallot, diced
4 tablespoons butter
½ cup grenadine liqueur
½ cup canned demi-glace

POTATO NESTS:

2 large Idaho potatoes
½ cup cornstarch
4 cups vegetable oil

1. Preheat oven to 300°F.

2. Start by making the potato nests. Peel and shred the potatoes, rinse in cold water, then strain. Add cornstarch, mixing until the shredded potatoes are coated evenly.

3. Use a deep fryer or large pot to heat oil on high heat. Coat the inside of a large ladle with a layer of potato mixture. Place a smaller ladle inside the large ladle with the layer of potato mixture in between, then insert both into the hot oil. Fry for 2 minutes, remove the small ladle, and then continue to fry the potato nest for an additional 2 minutes.

4. Carefully remove nest and set to the side. Repeat with the rest of the potato mixture.

5. Coat the duck legs with the fresh garlic, rosemary, salt, and pepper and bake in a pan for 2 hours.

6. While duck is baking, prepare the sauce.

7. Sauté the shallot in butter and add grenadine liqueur. Reduce by half and add demi-glace.

8. Place potato nest in center of plate. Place a duck leg inside the nest. Garnish with microgreens and grenadine liqueur, and then drizzle with sauce and serve.

photo by Lyle Okihara

ESCARGOT RAVIOLI Serves 4

This recipe is one of my most recent creations that I prepared on my birthday for a dinner party. As a lover of escargots and someone who grew up in France and Italy, I can't think of a better marriage than combining escargots with pasta. The garlic butter with parsley creates an amazing fragrance in the dining room of the restaurant when the ravioli is served.

RAVIOLI:

2 tablespoons salted butter

1 tablespoon diced shallots

10 large cloves of garlic, grated (preferably fresh)

8 escargots

2 tablespoons chopped fresh parsley

Pinch crushed red chili flakes

Salt and pepper to taste

¼ cup Pernod liquor (or anisette flavor substitute)

16 (4-inch) round wonton wrappers

1½ tablespoons cleaned and blanched spinach

2 egg yolks, lightly beaten (set aside in small bowl)

SAUCE:

2 tablespoons unsalted butter

Pinch of fresh shallot, minced

Pinch fresh garlic, minced

½ cup white wine

1 cup cream

Splash lemon juice

Salt and pepper to taste

1. Add butter to medium-sized saucepan over medium heat. Add shallots and garlic. Cook for 2 minutes. Then add escargots and cook for 2 more minutes.

2. Add parsley, chili flakes, salt, and pepper. Add Pernod and cook until reduced by half. Remove from heat and set aside.

3. Lay 8 wonton wrappers on a flat workspace. Add approximately ½ teaspoon spinach to center of each wonton wrapper and 1 cooked and shelled escargot.

4. Brush edges of wonton wrapper with egg yolk. Then place another wonton wrapper over the escargot to make the ravioli. Press sides of ravioli together firmly to seal edges. Place in salted boiling water for 3 minutes. Set aside.

5. Place butter, shallot, garlic, and white wine in a sauté pan. When the butter is melted and the garlic is fragrant, add cream and reduce to ¾ cup. Add a splash of lemon juice and salt and pepper to taste.

6. Reheat ravioli in salted boiling water for 1 minute then drain and place on a plate, finishing with sauce on top.

photo courtesy of Dan Zigler Photography

HEIRLOOM TOMATO SALAD (CAPRESE SALAD) Serves 4

Caprese is one of the most classic Italian salads, but when it's prepared with burrata cheese it gives the Caprese an extra touch of panache. Burrata is made from an outer layer of mozzarella cheese and filled with stracciatella and cream.

TOMATO SALAD:

12 ounces fresh burrata

1 large red onion (enough for 8 slices)

8 fresh red tomatoes

8 yellow tomatoes

Pinch of chopped parsley

DRESSING:

½ cup + 2 tablespoons balsamic vinegar

¼ cup + 2 tablespoons Passion Fruit
   and Ginger "House" Dressing
   (see below)

1 cup olive oil

2 tablespoons lemon juice

Salt and pepper to taste

PASSION FRUIT AND GINGER "HOUSE" DRESSING

(Makes approximately 10 ounces)

1 egg yolk*

1 tablespoon granulated sugar

2 tablespoons passion fruit puree

1 tablespoon Japanese pink ginger,
   pureed

2 tablespoons rice wine vinegar

1 cup extra-virgin olive oil

1. In a large mixing bowl, combine egg yolk and sugar.

2. Slowly stir in passion fruit puree, ginger, and rice wine vinegar until smooth in consistency.

3. Slowly whisk in olive oil.**
Chill and serve.

Warning: Please be aware that consuming raw egg yolks can increase the risk of food borne illnesses.

**Hint: Adding olive oil all at once will cause dressing to "break."*

Use approximately 2 tablespoons of dressing per handful of greens if using in other salads.

photo courtesy of Dan Zigler Photography

LOBSTER RAVIOLI WITH CITRUS SAUCE (A.K.A. GWEN STEFANI RAVIOLI) Serves 2

When famous singer Gwen Stefani, originally from Anaheim, had a family dinner at our restaurant, I decided to create a special appetizer, which we named after her. The orange mixed with ginger gives the ravioli a nice bite. Today it has become one of the top sellers on our menu.

CITRUS SAUCE:

8 tablespoons unsalted butter, cubed and chilled, divided

1 shallot, diced

½ cup orange liqueur

1½ cups orange juice

½ cup heavy whipping cream

RAVIOLI:

3 ounces lobster meat

9 ounces raw shrimp, peeled and cleaned

1 ounce sushi ginger

1 tablespoon fresh basil, minced

Salt and pepper

16 wonton wrappers

2 egg whites, lightly beaten

1. Prepare the sauce. Melt 2 tablespoons of butter in a sauté pan over medium heat. Add the shallots and sauté for 2 minutes. Add the orange liqueur and simmer until reduced by half. Add the orange juice and simmer until the mixture is reduced by half again.

2. Remove the sauce from the heat and whisk in the cream and the remaining cold butter.

3. In a food processor, combine the lobster, shrimp, ginger, basil, ½ cup of the citrus sauce, and salt and pepper. Pulse the mixture until smooth.

4. To assemble the ravioli, lay 8 of the wonton wrappers on a work surface and top each wrapper with a tablespoon of the lobster mousse. Brush the edges of the wonton wrappers with the beaten egg, and then place another wonton skin on top of each wrapper and press the sides together firmly to seal the edges. Refrigerate for 30 minutes to let egg wash seal firmly.

5. Bring a large pot of salted water to a boil. Drop the lobster ravioli into the boiling water and cook for 2 minutes.

6. Place four ravioli on each of the serving plates. Top with the remaining citrus sauce.

photo courtesy of Dan Zigler Photography

PORTOBELLO MUSHROOM RAVIOLI Serves 2

Mushrooms remind me of when I used to pick them in France with my Uncle Rodolfo in a forest near my house. I think they were porcini mushrooms. It is a great memory from my childhood. Because I have such a love of mushrooms, this is one of my favorite ravioli dishes.

6 tablespoons butter, divided

2 tablespoons diced shallot

¼ cup brandy

¼ cup heavy cream

¼ cup canned demi-glace

1 tablespoon extra-virgin olive oil

2 ounces white mushrooms, cut in halves

4 cups fresh spinach

Salt and pepper to taste

8 large frozen portobello mushroom and spinach ravioli

2 tablespoons green peppercorns

1. Melt 2 tablespoons of butter in a pan. Add shallots, and sauté until golden brown.

2. Add brandy and flambé.

3. Add heavy cream, demi-glace, and remaining butter and cook until the butter has melted. Remove from heat and place into a blender to thicken.

4. In a large skillet heat olive oil, then add mushrooms and spinach and cook over medium heat for approximately 4 minutes. Add salt and pepper to taste.

5. In a separate large pot, bring salted water to a boil and add ravioli. Cook approximately 5 minutes or until tender. Drain well.

6. On two large plates spread mushrooms and spinach in the center of each plate. Add cooked ravioli on top, and top with sauce and peppercorns.

photo courtesy of Dan Zigler Photography

SCALLOPS WITH BEET MASHED POTATOES

Serves 2

Mamma Caterina worked very hard for seventeen years in the north of France picking beets. This dish reminds me of her hard work in the farmlands. Beets have a unique flavor that is both sweet and bitter, and I love to work with this veggie because of the great color it lends to the plate.

BEET MASHED POTATOES:

2 large potatoes

1 tablespoon butter, divided

Salt and pepper to taste

¼ cup cream

½ cup milk

1 medium beet, boiled or roasted
   and then pureed

SAUCE:

1 large shallot, diced

1 ripe mango, peeled and diced

½ cup white wine

2 ounces sushi ginger

½ cup manufacturing cream

8 fresh scallops

½ cup microgreens (to garnish)

1. Preheat the oven to 350° F.

2. For the Beet Mashed Potatoes, boil the potatoes for around 10 to 20 minutes until soft. Drain potatoes and mash, then add butter, salt, cream, milk, and beet puree. Place in a pastry bag and cover with aluminum foil to keep hot.

3. For the sauce, place shallots, diced mango, wine, sushi ginger, and manufacturing cream in a small sauté pan. Cook until reduced by about one-half. Puree in a blender then strain.

4. In a sauté pan sear both sides of the scallops until golden brown and tender. Then place in the oven for 5 minutes.

5. For the presentation, serve the Beet Mashed Potatoes on a plate, place the scallops on top, and drizzle with mango sauce. Garnish with microgreens.

photo by Lyle Okihara

SMOKED SALMON Serves 4

Smoked salmon reminds me of Christmas Eve. My sister Flavia often pre-pared it on that occasion. Otherwise I rarely saw this dish in my first twenty-five years because of the price. You can use smoked salmon in many different dishes for amazing flavor.

12 ounces sliced Norwegian
    smoked salmon

2 tablespoons salmon caviar

2 tablespoons chopped red onion

2 tablespoons diced chives

2 tablespoons olive oil

Pepper to taste

¼ cup crème fraîche

¼ cup sliced radish

1. Divide all ingredients into four portions, starting with the salmon. Lay three slices of salmon on each plate, slightly staggered, and then roll into a rose shape. Place in the center of the plate and garnish with all remaining ingredients.

photo courtesy of Dan Zigler Photography

STUFFED CALAMARI Serves 4

I created my recipe for stuffed calamari to offer a unique presentation of this popular seafood, which is traditionally fried. The fresh herbs, crabmeat, and caper sauce make this an elegant dish with a rich flavor.

BÉCHAMEL SAUCE:

½ cup unsalted butter
½ cup diced shallot
¼ cup all-purpose flour
¾ cup whole milk
Pinch of nutmeg
Salt and pepper to taste

CALAMARI:

Pinch of minced garlic
2 tablespoons parsley
Pinch of fresh chopped tarragon
1 pound lump crabmeat
2 pounds Dungeness crabmeat
4 (5-ounce) calamari steaks
3 whole eggs, beaten
¼ cup all-purpose flour

CAPER SAUCE:

½ cup + 2 tablespoons
   unsalted butter
1 small shallot, diced
1 cup white wine
2 tablespoons lemon juice
1 tablespoon chopped parsley
1 teaspoon capers
Salt and pepper to taste

1. Preheat the oven to 375° F.

2. Start the béchamel sauce. Place the butter in a medium-sized pot. Once melted add the diced shallot, and then gradually add flour to create a thick roux.

3. In a separate pan, heat milk at a low temperature. Gradually add milk to the roux. Cook until reduced by about one-half, then add pinch of nutmeg, and salt and pepper to taste.

4. In a large bowl, combine garlic, parsley, tarragon, lump crab, and Dungeness crabmeat. Add béchamel sauce gradually until mixture is moist and malleable.

5. Place calamari steaks on a sheet of plastic wrap, cover with another sheet of plastic wrap, and tenderize. Remove top layer of plastic wrap, while leaving bottom layer intact. Spoon crab filling onto calamari steaks and roll, using the bottom layer of plastic wrap to keep the filling and calamari intact. Remove plastic when calamari is completely rolled.

6. Dip the stuffed calamari in egg and dust with flour. Brown in nonstick pan. Then bake approximately 12 minutes in preheated oven.

7. While the calamari is cooking, start the caper sauce. In a small saucepan, combine 2 tablespoons unsalted butter, the shallot, and white wine. Cook until reduced by one-half, and then add the remaining butter and lemon juice. Finish with chopped parsley, capers, salt, and pepper.

8. Take the calamari out of the oven, place each steak on a plate, slice, drizzle with caper sauce, and serve.

photo by Lyle Okihara

TORTELLINI CATERINA Serves 4

Mamma Caterina always prepared a nice espresso when someone walked through the door, as many Italian families do. Adding espresso to tortellini or ravioli reminds me of Mamma Caterina offering an espresso to anyone who visited. The bittersweet espresso sauce makes this a lovely addition to the tortellini.

1 tablespoon salt

1 teaspoon olive oil

24 pieces of large cheese tortellini

½ cup Marsala wine

¼ cup brewed espresso

½ cup coffee

Dash of cream

8 tablespoons butter

3 tablespoons granulated sugar

4 edible orchid flowers

Fresh Italian parsley

1. Boil 2 quarts of water with 1 tablespoon salt and 1 teaspoon olive oil. Cook tortellini until tender. Drain well.

2. In a saucepan, heat wine, espresso, and coffee. Reduce by one-third. Add the dash of cream and the butter and sugar. Stir until sugar has completely dissolved.

3. Spoon a few tablespoons of sauce on each plate and place 6 tortellini atop sauce. Garnish with orchid and parsley and serve.

photo by Lyle Okihara

ENTREES

BRAISED SHORT RIBS Serves 2

This dish reminds me of Mamma Caterina, who used to make an Italian style of braised beef called brasato often. I had to put it on my menu. It is a touch of Mamma Caterina's food, which was influenced by the peasant food of the region where I grew up in Italy. I often pair it with polenta, which is now served in some of the finest restaurants in the world. (If you'd like to serve polenta with your ribs, see Filet Mignon with Gorgonzola Cheese *on page 178 for the recipe.)*

RIBS:

2 pounds boneless short ribs

Salt and pepper to taste

8 cups canned demi-glace

4 bay leaves

MUSHROOM SAUCE:

2 tablespoons butter

1 large shallot, minced

1 cup sliced portobello mushrooms

1 cup shiitake mushrooms

1 cup heavy cream

½ cup canned demi-glace

Salt and pepper

Fresh thyme

1. To cook short ribs, preheat oven to 275° F. Cut rib meat from bones and roll and tie with string. In sauté pan, sear both sides, add salt and pepper, and place in a baking pan. Add demi-glace and bay leaves. Braise for 3 hours.

2. To make mushroom sauce, preheat a sauté pan over medium heat. Add butter and shallot and cook for 1 minute. Add mushrooms and cook until golden brown. Add cream, demi-glace, salt, pepper, and thyme. Reduce for 5 minutes on low heat.

3. To serve, place short rib on a dinner plate and top with mushroom sauce. Garnish with fresh herbs and/or edible flowers (optional).

photo by Lyle Okihara

173

BRAISED RABBIT Serves 4

When I was growing up my parents raised rabbits in our backyard. I used to clean the rabbits with Mom, which was not a pleasant thing to do, but she often cooked rabbit on Sunday. Sometimes she made pâté of rabbit, which is called pâté de lapin *in France, and still today it is my favorite pâté in the world. This dish has become one of my favorite meat dishes. I love the taste and flavor—and don't forget to enjoy it with a piece of bread if you decide to make a pâté with the braised rabbit meat!*

1 whole rabbit, skinned and
  broken down

Salt and pepper to taste

2 tablespoons olive oil

2 cups finely diced leeks

2 cups finely diced onions

6 garlic cloves, minced

1 large carrot, peeled and diced

2 tablespoons rosemary,
  roughly chopped

1 cup chopped canned tomatoes

½ cup dry white wine

1. Preheat oven to 375° F.

2. Season rabbit with salt and pepper.

3. Heat olive oil in a heavy-based frying pan with a lid on medium-high. Lightly brown rabbit for 3 minutes on each side.

4. Add leeks, onions, garlic, carrots, and rosemary. Add chopped tomatoes and wine, and allow to reduce for 1 minute.

5. Ladle mixture evenly over the rabbit.

6. Cover the dish and bake for 1 hour in the oven. Let sit for 10 minutes before serving.

photo courtesy of Dan Zigler Photography

CHEESE RAVIOLI WITH PORCINI MUSHROOM SAUCE Serves 2

Growing up in Italy, cheese ravioli is a popular Sunday feast item that is also loved by the American palate. The porcini mushroom sauce is one of my favorites. You'll feel like you are in a forest when you eat this earthy dish.

2 ounces dried porcini mushrooms

2 tablespoons unsalted butter

1 whole shallot, diced

½ cup brandy

2 cups heavy whipping cream

Salt and pepper to taste

18 cheese-filled ravioli

2 tablespoons olive oil

Sprigs of fresh micro greens

1. Soak porcini mushrooms in water for 30 minutes.

2. Melt butter in a saucepan on low to medium heat, add shallots, and cook until golden brown.

3. Add brandy and reduce by half.

4. Add mushrooms and cream, and cook over low heat for 8 minutes.

5. Remove sauce from heat and puree in a blender. Add salt and pepper to taste.

6. Bring water to a boil and add ravioli, olive oil, and salt. Cook for 5 minutes or until the pasta is tender.

7. Using a ladle, spread sauce on a long plate, and then top with 9 ravioli, laying them side by side, slightly overlapping.

8. Garnish each plate with a few sprigs of fresh greens.

photo by Lyle Okihara

FILET MIGNON WITH GORGONZOLA CHEESE Serves 4

Traditional beef tenderloin can be served in many ways. Gorgonzola cheese is a blue cheese I love that's produced mainly in the north of Italy. There are two varieties: Gorgonzola Piccante and Gorgonzola Dolce (meaning Sweet Gorgonzola), the younger version that is soft, creamy, and sweet. I decided to try it with filet mignon and it turned out to be a wonderful creation.

FILET MIGNON:

2 cups canned demi-glace

3 ounces gorgonzola cheese

4 (8-ounce) filet mignon cuts

POLENTA:

14 ounces or 1¾ cups water

¾ cup instant polenta

6 tablespoons butter

1 cup 2 percent milk

Salt and pepper to taste

1. Preheat oven to 350° F.

2. Prepare the polenta. Bring water to a boil and add polenta, butter, and milk. Stir with a wooden spoon until all ingredients are combined. Add salt and pepper. Remove from heat, spread polenta onto a wax paper sheet, and allow to cool. Using a circular cookie cutter, cut out one circle of polenta for each serving.

3. Simmer demi-glace for the filet mignon in a saucepan until reduced by one-fourth. Slowly add gorgonzola crumbles until they are half dissolved. Remove from heat.

4. Brown both sides of each filet in a sauté pan, and then bake approximately 8 minutes for rare, 12 minutes for medium rare, 15 minutes for medium, 16 minutes for medium well, and 18 minutes for well done.

5. Place each filet atop polenta, and top with gorgonzola demi-glace and serve.

photo by Lyle Okihara

GNOCCHI WITH GORGONZOLA CHEESE SAUCE Serves 2

Verona, my hometown, is world famous for gnocchi and has an annual festival celebrating this pasta. Gnocchi was my mother's favorite dish from as far back as I can remember. She would wake up early on Sundays to make them. Her special recipe included sugar, cinnamon, and brown butter, which is still my favorite today. But for the American palate I decided to add gorgonzola instead as a sauce and a touch of tomato for color.

16 ounces premade potato gnocchi

¾ cup heavy cream

4 ounces (½ cup) gorgonzola cheese

½ cup tomato sauce

Salt and pepper to taste

1. To cook the gnocchi, bring salted water to a boil in large pot. Add gnocchi. Gnocchi are cooked when they rise to the top (approximately 2 minutes). Drain and set aside.

2. For the cheese sauce, heat cream over low heat. Add gorgonzola cheese and cook until mixture is creamy and cheese is melted. Add tomato sauce and bring to a boil. Season with salt and pepper to taste (being careful to not over salt).

3. Toss cooked gnocchi in sauce and serve.

photo courtesy of Dan Zigler Photography

ITALIAN BRANZINO Serves 2

Branzino is the most popular fish in the Mediterranean, and it has been extremely popular in America the past few years. The reason why I love this fish is that it doesn't need much of anything, because it possesses outstanding flavor all on its own. It tastes and feels like you are sitting by the Mediterranean Sea when you experience the flavors in this dish.

2 (1-pound) whole Mediterranean sea bass, cleaned, deboned, heads off, tails intact

2 tablespoons extra-virgin olive oil, divided

Kosher salt

Freshly ground pepper

1 cup red cherry tomato halves

1 cup yellow cherry tomato halves

1 lemon

1. Rub fish with one tablespoon olive oil and season with kosher salt and pepper.

2. Place fish inside steamer (if fish is too large, bend slightly, making sure not to touch water). Bring water to a boil over high heat and steam for approximately 5 minutes.

3. In a medium-sized skillet, heat remaining olive oil to medium heat. Add tomatoes and sauté for 2 minutes.

4. Place steamed fish on large plates and top with half of the tomatoes per plate. Squeeze the juice from cut whole lemon over fish and serve.

photo courtesy of Dan Zigler Photography

KALE RAVIOLI* IN MANGO SAUCE Serves 2

This recipe is another new item on my menu that just so happens to be gluten free. Gluten-free dishes have been a major request by many of our patrons, and you can now find gluten-free ravioli in most health food stores and many major supermarkets. These ravioli are extremely delicate, and adding mango sauce adds a tropical touch that reminds me of Hawaii.

1 cup frozen mango puree

½ cup agave nectar

2 tablespoons water

16 frozen kale and ricotta gluten-free ravioli

2 tablespoons chopped parsley

1. In a medium-sized skillet over medium heat liquefy the frozen mango puree. Then add the agave nectar and water and reduce by half.

2. Boil the ravioli according to the instructions in a large pot of salted water until tender. Drain well.

3. Pour the mango sauce on a large plate and place the ravioli over the sauce. Garnish and sprinkle with chopped parsley.

*gluten free

photo courtesy of Dan Zigler Photography

LINGUINE WITH CHIVE PESTO Serves 4

Pesto sauce originated in Genoa, a city in Northern Italy, and is one of the most famous traditional sauces in all of Italy. To add a different touch, I decided to use chives and shallots instead of basil. I also added cream and removed the pine nuts for those who have allergies.

1 pound dry linguine pasta

4 cups heavy whipping cream

2 teaspoons extra-virgin olive oil

10 large cloves fresh garlic, diced

2 large shallots, peeled and diced

½ cup diced fresh chives

4 ounces (½ cup) fresh Grana
    Padano cheese, grated

Salt and pepper to taste

1. Cook pasta for 12 minutes or until tender. Set aside.

2. Heat the cream in a large saucepan over low heat. Watch it carefully and do not let it come to a boil.

3. While the cream is warming, heat olive oil in a small sauté pan and brown the garlic and shallots; remove from heat.

4. In a blender, puree the cooked shallots, garlic, olive oil, and chives.

5. Add the chive mixture to the heated cream and simmer for 5 minutes or until slightly reduced. Add cheese and salt and pepper to taste.

6. Toss the cooked pasta with the chive pesto and serve. Garnish with extra cheese if desired.

photo by Lyle Okihara

LOBSTER CIOPPINO Serves 2

Cioppino is a dish similar to many found throughout the Mediterranean. Because of its mélange of seafood, I feel it represents Italy very well, as Italy is surrounded by the sea. Venice is my favorite city in the world by the sea, and cioppino reminds me of that city.

3 tablespoons extra-virgin olive oil, divided

1 tablespoon chopped garlic

10 black mussels

6 medium-sized shrimp

¼ pound calamari squid rings

4 Venus clams

¼ pound fresh whitefish, cut into chunks

½ cup tomato sauce

½ cup white wine

1 cup seafood broth

1 tablespoon chopped fresh basil

Salt and pepper to taste

2 (4-ounce) lobster tails, cleaned

1 tablespoon unsalted butter

4 ounces cooked capellini pasta

Pinch of paprika

1. Preheat oven to 350° F.

2. Heat 2 tablespoons of the olive oil in a large sauté pan over medium high heat and add the garlic, cooking until browned.

3. Add all seafood (except lobster), tomato sauce, wine, seafood broth, and basil, and season with salt and pepper. Cook for approximately 12 minutes or until clams and mussels are fully opened.

4. Loosen lobster meat from shell, but do not fully remove by leaving end of tail intact. Leave meat on top of shell and lightly rub the top of the lobster meat with butter, and sprinkle with salt, pepper, and paprika. Bake for approximately 5 minutes or until cooked through.

5. Boil 1 quart of salted water with the remaining tablespoon of olive oil and cook pasta for 2 minutes.

6. In two large bowls place half the pasta at the bottom, top with the seafood mixture, and top off with a lobster tail.

photo by Lyle Okihara

LOBSTER TAILS Serves 2

I'd never had a lobster until I came to America at the age of almost twenty-five. The first one I remember well was at a restaurant where I used to work called La Vie en Rose, where they served Lobster Thermidor. It was one of the restaurant's best sellers. Even today, at my restaurant, it has become an almost weekly special. The champagne sauce is delicate and perfect on top of the lobster.

6 (4- to 5-ounce) Atlantic lobster tails

1 cup butter (2 sticks), divided

2 whole shallots, diced

2 cups champagne

1 teaspoon cream

Salt and pepper to taste

1 teaspoon chopped parsley

1. Bring a large pot of water to a boil, add the lobster, and boil for 10 minutes. Remove the lobster, then carefully remove the meat from the tails using a knife or scissors (save the tails for later). Set lobster meat to the side, and just before serving, cook the meat an additional 2 minutes in boiling water.

2. Melt 1 stick of butter in a saucepan on low to medium heat. Add shallots and cook until golden brown. Add champagne and cook until the sauce is reduced by half. Add the cream and the remaining stick of butter.

3. After the sauce has a consistent texture, pour into a blender and puree. Add salt and pepper to taste, and finish with chopped parsley.

4. Place lobster meat on top of the lobster tails on the plate. Drizzle sauce on top and serve.

photo courtesy of Dan Zigler Photography

MAMMA'S SPAGHETTI MARINARA

Makes enough for 4 entrée servings

I ate spaghetti prepared by Mamma Caterina Monday through Friday for lunch for almost twenty years. This was because it was the most affordable food that Mom and Dad could buy. I ate it to the point that, at one time, I hated it. Today, Mamma's Spaghetti Marinara has been served to more than one million hungry children in need of food. I call this Mamma Caterina's #1 family dish, and today I love it. My memory of this meal is seeing Mom waiting by the window for her kids to come home from school so she could begin cooking Spaghetti Marinara (tears!).

1 tablespoon olive oil

1½ teaspoons minced garlic

1 pound peeled tomatoes

1 quart tomato sauce

¾ teaspoon salt

½ teaspoon black pepper

¼ cup fresh chopped basil

¼ cup fresh chopped parsley

2 tablespoons kosher salt

1 pound spaghetti pasta

1. Place oil, garlic, tomatoes, tomato sauce, regular salt, and pepper in a medium hot skillet and bring it to the boiling point. Turn down the heat and allow to simmer for 25 minutes, stirring occasionally. At the last minute stir in the basil and parsley.

2. For the pasta, bring 5 quarts of water to a boil in a large pot. Add 2 tablespoons kosher salt. Add 1 pound of spaghetti or other pasta and cook until barely al dente, about 10 minutes.

3. Drain pasta and place on a serving dish. Pour the sauce over the cooked pasta and serve with grated Parmesan cheese, if desired.

photo courtesy of Dan Zigler Photography

NEW YORK STEAK Serves 2

Americans love meat, and a New York steak is a "must-have" on the menu.
I never had the privilege of tasting one until I was twenty-five years old. Dried,
unripe green peppercorns from Madagascar give the steak a great nuance, and
people love our brandy cream sauce.

SAUCE:

4 tablespoons unsalted butter, divided
1 teaspoon sliced shallots
¼ cup brandy
¼ cup manufacturing cream
¼ cup demi-glace

STEAKS:

2 (12-ounce) bone-in New York steaks
¼ cup extra-virgin olive oil
Ground black pepper to taste
1 teaspoon green peppercorns

1. Preheat oven to 350° F.

2. Melt 2 tablespoons of butter in a pan and sauté shallots until golden brown.

3. Add brandy and flambé. When the flame is gone, add cream and reduce by half. Add demi-glace and remaining butter. Place sauce in a blender to thicken.

4. Brush the steaks with extra-virgin olive oil and ground pepper. Place in a preheated pan and sear each side until golden brown (approximately 30 seconds to 1 minute.)

5. Place the pan in the oven and cook the steaks until desired temperature is reached. When desired temperature is reached, let steak "rest" with no heat for 3 minutes.

6. Serve the steaks with sauce and peppercorns.

photo courtesy of Lyle Okihara

195

PAPPARDELLE BOLOGNESE Serves 4

I love this dish because the texture of pappardelle stays al dente, the way Italians love to eat pasta, and this was well received at my restaurant. The Bologna region is considered the capital of Italian food and is where the delicious Bolognese sauce originates.

¼ cup olive oil

1 cup chopped onion

½ cup chopped celery

½ cup chopped carrot

4 garlic cloves, minced

1 pound ground beef

1 cup red wine

1½ cups canned tomato puree

14 ounces canned beef broth

2 bay leaves

Salt and pepper to taste

1 pound pappardelle pasta

Freshly grated Parmesan cheese

1. Heat oil in a large pot over medium-high heat. Add onion, celery, carrots, and garlic. Sauté 5 minutes.

2. Add ground beef. Sauté until browned and cooked throughout, breaking up meat with the back of a fork, for approximately 10 minutes.

3. Add wine, tomato puree, beef broth, and bay leaves. Reduce heat to medium low. Simmer until sauce thickens, stirring often for approximately 1 hour, while seasoning with salt and pepper to taste. Remove bay leaves.

4. Boil pasta in a large pot of salted water until tender but still firm to bite, around 10 minutes, stirring often. Drain.

5. Transfer pasta to sauce, toss, and serve. Garnish with Parmesan.

photo courtesy of Dan Zigler Photography

PASTA CALABRESE* Serves 4

Calabria is a region in Southern Italy where a variety of vegetables are grown. This dish reminds me of close friends from that region, where vegetables were a mainstay on the dinner table. This dish is like eating outside in your garden.

14 ounces dry wheat linguine

8 stalks green asparagus

10 snow peas

1 tablespoon diced fresh garlic

5 ounces yellow cherry tomatoes

5 ounces red cherry tomatoes

2 tablespoons fresh sweet basil

3 ounces Parmesan cheese, grated

Salt and pepper to taste

1. Bring 3 quarts of water to a boil. Add 1 tablespoon olive oil and 1 tablespoon salt. Add pasta and cook for 10 minutes or until pasta is tender. Drain well.

2. Cook asparagus and snow peas in the same boiling water that was used for the pasta until your desired texture is achieved.

3. In a sauté pan add the rest of the olive oil, fresh garlic, yellow tomatoes, red tomatoes, and sweet basil and cook over medium-high heat for 2 minutes. Add cooked pasta, Parmesan, salt, and pepper.

4. Garnish with cooked green asparagus and snow peas.

* Vegetarian

photo by Lyle Okihara

PENNE ALLA VODKA Serves 4-6

After a trip with my two sisters and brother to Moscow, I decided to add vodka to one of my pasta dishes. It turned out to be a great combination with tomato sauce.

1 tablespoon salt

1 tablespoon olive oil

1 pound dry penne pasta

6 tablespoons unsalted butter, divided

1 shallot, peeled and diced

¾ cup heavy cream

½ cup tomato sauce

1½ cups vodka

Salt and pepper to taste

1. Bring 1 gallon of water to boil with the salt and olive oil. Add pasta and cook for approximately 8 minutes, stirring occasionally until pasta is cooked to preferred tenderness. Remove from heat and strain.

2. While the pasta is cooking, melt 2 tablespoons of butter in a large sauté pan over medium heat. Add shallot and cook until translucent.

3. Add cream, tomato sauce, and vodka, and reduce by half. Add salt and pepper to taste and then add the remaining 4 tablespoons of butter.

4. Toss the sauce with the pasta and serve.

photo courtesy of Dan Zigler Photography

PENNE AMATRICIANA Serves 3-4

The name Amatriciana comes from a town in Lazio, the region where Rome is located, called Amatrice. This dish is dear to me because many of the chefs of Amatrice over the centuries were chefs to the popes. In 2016 the town of Amatrice was destroyed by a major earthquake, but the tradition of this recipe will never die. All the ingredients of Penne Amatriciana give this pasta a unique flavor loved by many. Historically pork cheeks were used in this dish, but instead I have used bacon. Pecorino cheese was also traditionally used, but because of the strong flavor, some people prefer Parmesan.

2 tablespoons table salt

1 pound dry penne pasta

1 pound uncooked smoked bacon, diced

2 medium yellow onions, chopped

8 ounces tomato sauce

¾ teaspoon crushed red chili

Basil and parsley to taste

Salt and pepper to taste

Pecorino or Parmesan cheese to taste

1. Bring water and salt to a boil in a pot. Add the pasta and cook, stirring occasionally, for approximately 8 minutes, or until preferred tenderness. Remove from heat and strain.

2. For the sauce, cook bacon in a sauté pan over medium heat for approximately 3 minutes. Add onions and cook for a few more minutes, then finally add the tomato sauce and cook for a few minutes more.

3. When the sauce is ready, add the cooked pasta and crushed red chili to taste. Garnish with basil and parsley. Top with Pecorino or Parmesan cheese.

photo courtesy of Dan Zigler Photography

POACHED SALMON AU CHOCOLAT Serves 2

I invented white chocolate mashed potatoes by mistake. While working in the kitchen, I had a piece of white chocolate in my hand. On the line was freshly made, hot mashed potatoes. I used the piece of white chocolate as a spoon to try the quality of the mashed potatoes. It melted in my mouth, and I realized something amazing could be created. After trying this out with a few dishes, I realized the perfect combination was pairing these potatoes with salmon.

SALMON:

½ gallon water
1 small carrot, chopped
½ onion, chopped
2 tablespoons lemon juice
2 tablespoons salt
16 ounces (1 pound) fresh salmon

WHITE CHOCOLATE MASHED POTATOES:

1 pound russet potatoes, cleaned
    and peeled
4 ounces white chocolate
4 tablespoons unsalted butter
Pinch of salt

CITRUS SAUCE:

8 tablespoons unsalted butter,
    divided
1 shallot, diced
½ cup orange liqueur
½ cup heavy whipping cream
1½ cups orange juice

1. Combine water, carrot, onion, lemon juice, and salt in a large pan and bring to a simmer. Add salmon and simmer for 12 minutes.

2. Boil potatoes until soft, and then drain. Using a double boiler, melt the white chocolate. Add the melted chocolate to the potatoes and mash. Add butter and salt, and continue to mash until texture is consistent.

3. For the sauce, melt 2 tablespoons of the butter in a sauté pan, add the shallots, and cook for 2 minutes. Add orange liqueur and reduce by half. Add orange juice and reduce by half again. Add remaining butter and cream and cook until butter is melted.

4. Remove the salmon from the pan, serve atop the mashed potatoes, and top with citrus sauce.

photo by Lyle Okihara

205

PRAWNS AND SCALLOPS Serves 4

Prawns are a popular item on many Italian menus, and they always remind me of the Adriatic Sea. In the city of Pescara, where my brother used to play professional soccer, prawns were always served at the table. Scallops with soy sauce were an extra touch. Speaking of soccer, I had the privilege of meeting my idol Roberto Baggio—the number one Italian soccer player and world soccer champion—in Milan. I went to a few of his matches to see him play, and it was like watching someone skating across the soccer field. I was even invited to his house for dinner where I touched the FIFA Golden Ball that he received for "player of the year."

SALMON:

½ gallon water

1 small carrot, chopped

½ onion, chopped

2 tablespoons lemon juice

2 tablespoons salt

16 ounces (1 pound) fresh salmon

WHITE CHOCOLATE MASHED POTATOES:

1 pound russet potatoes, cleaned and peeled

4 ounces white chocolate

4 tablespoons unsalted butter

Pinch of salt

CITRUS SAUCE:

8 tablespoons unsalted butter, divided

1 shallot, diced

½ cup orange liqueur

½ cup heavy whipping cream

1½ cups orange juice

1. Combine water, carrot, onion, lemon juice, and salt in a large pan and bring to a simmer. Add salmon and simmer for 12 minutes.

2. Boil potatoes until soft, and then drain. Using a double boiler, melt the white chocolate. Add the melted chocolate to the potatoes and mash. Add butter and salt, and continue to mash until texture is consistent.

3. For the sauce, melt 2 tablespoons of the butter in a sauté pan, add the shallots, and cook for 2 minutes. Add orange liqueur and reduce by half. Add orange juice and reduce by half again. Add remaining butter and cream and cook until butter is melted.

4. Remove the salmon from the pan, serve atop the mashed potatoes, and top with citrus sauce.

photo by Lyle Okihara

RACK OF LAMB Serves 4

Lamb has a wonderful, delicate flavor and often makes me think of childhood memories. It reminds me especially of watching the sun go down as Mamma Caterina's father, Nonno Giovanni, the Shepherd of Villanova, returned home with a herd of one hundred sheep.

Lamb scraps (optional)

1 sprig fresh rosemary

1 shallot, diced

1 tablespoon chopped garlic

½ cup white wine

½ cup demi-glace

Salt and pepper to taste

2 teaspoons olive oil

3 pounds Australian or New Zealand rack of lamb, cut into chops

1. Preheat oven to 350° F.

2. Sauté lamb scraps (if available) until golden, add rosemary, shallot, garlic, and white wine, and cook until reduced by about half. Add demi-glace and reduce to one-quarter.

3. Strain through cheesecloth and season with salt and black pepper.

4. Add olive oil to a sauté pan. Season both sides of each chop with salt and pepper, place in a sauté pan, and put into the oven. Oven roast to your preference or approximately 8 minutes for rare, 12 minutes for medium rare, 15 minutes for medium, 16 minutes for medium well, and 18 minutes for well done.

5. Plate chops and drizzle with previously prepared sauce.

photo by Lyle Okihara

RIGATONI CARBONARA Serves 4

This dish was created in the middle of the twentieth century. I personally prepared this dish often at the age of sixteen for our Italian customers late in the evening, almost like a midnight snack. Still today, Rigatoni Carbonara is one of the most famous dishes of Rome.

2 tablespoons salt

1 tablespoon olive oil

1 pound dry rigatoni pasta

7 large egg yolks

1 large egg

8 ounces pancetta, cut into
⅓-inch cubes

½ cup finely grated Parmigiano-
Reggiano cheese, plus additional
for topping

2 teaspoons ground black pepper

1. Bring 1 gallon of water with salt and olive oil to a boil. Add pasta and cook for approximately 8–10 minutes, stirring occasionally, until pasta is cooked to preferred tenderness. Remove from heat and strain. Reserve some pasta water for sauce.

2. Whisk eggs together and set aside.

3. For the sauce, cook pancetta in a large skillet over medium-low heat, stirring frequently until fat renders but pancetta is not brown (about 5 minutes). Pour through a fine mesh sieve into a bowl and reserve drippings.

4. Place rigatoni pasta into skillet and immediately add whisked eggs, 2 tablespoons of the drippings, and 1 tablespoon pancetta. Toss to coat, working in three batches. Gradually add ⅓ of the cheese at a time, stirring and tossing to melt between the batches. Add black pepper and toss until sauce thickens, adding reserved pasta cooking water in tablespoon increments if needed.

5. Divide pasta among dishes and add black pepper and cheese to taste, then serve.

photo by Navid Zadeh

SAND DABS Serves 4

This is a favorite dish of the ninety-year-old Bevin twins, two of our beautiful daily customers. Loved by many, this fish cannot be found in many places. It's so delicate that fish lovers are happy to see it back on my menu.

Olive oil

4 (7-ounce) filets of sand dabs, cleaned and boneless

6 tablespoons all-purpose flour

3 whole eggs, beaten

Pinch of chopped parsley

1 cup unsalted butter, divided

1 shallot, diced

1 cup Chardonnay wine

Dash of cream

2 tablespoons lemon juice

Salt and pepper to taste

1. Heat olive oil in a large nonstick sauté pan. Drizzle the sand dabs with all-purpose flour then dip into eggs. One at a time, cook sand dab filets for 2 minutes on each side, and then sprinkle with parsley.

2. Place half of the butter and diced shallots in a sauté pan and cook for 2 minutes. Add Chardonnay, and cook until reduced by about half. Add dash of cream and the remaining butter. Stir slowly, adding lemon juice, salt, and pepper.

3. Place sand dabs on a plate, drizzle with sauce, and serve.

photo by Lyle Okihara

SEARED AHI WITH TROPICAL RELISH Serves 2

I like this fish because of the beautiful, deep-red color. This dish is an amazing substitute for someone who does not eat red meat. The tropical relish makes it fresh and delicious.

2 tablespoons brown sugar

¼ cup + 2 tablespoons soy sauce

¼ cup rice wine vinegar

2 tablespoons diced fresh ginger

2 tablespoons water

½ cup diced fresh mango

½ cup diced fresh papaya

½ cup diced fresh strawberries

½ cup diced cucumber

1 pound ahi tuna steak

2 tablespoons paprika

2 tablespoons Cajun spice mix

Salt to taste

2 tablespoons extra-virgin olive oil

1. In a large bowl mix together brown sugar, soy sauce, rice wine vinegar, ginger, and water. Then add the fruits and cucumber to the bowl.

2. Coat ahi steak with paprika, Cajun spices, and salt. In a large skillet over medium-high heat, add olive oil and sauté ahi for 2 minutes on each side. Remove from pan and slice into ⅛-inch portions.

3. Place sliced tuna on two plates, top with fruit mixture, and serve.

photo by Lyle Okihara

SHRIMP SCAMPI Serves 4

Shrimp scampi has been a famous Italian dish for years and is a classic. Customers love when we mix pasta and seafood together. Pasta with shrimp is one of my favorite combos. The red pepper flakes in my shrimp scampi recipe give it a bit of an added kick.

1 pound angel hair pasta

2 tablespoons butter

2 tablespoons extra-virgin olive oil

4 garlic cloves, minced

½ cup dry white wine

⅛ teaspoon crushed
    red pepper flakes

1 pound large or extra-large
    uncooked shrimp, peeled

Juice of ½ lemon

⅓ cup chopped parsley

1. Boil angel hair pasta in a large pot of salted water until tender. Drain well and set aside.

2. In a large skillet, melt butter with olive oil on medium heat. Add garlic and sauté until fragrant (about 1 minute). Add wine and red pepper flakes and bring to a simmer. Let wine reduce by one-half (about 2 minutes). Add shrimp and sauté until they turn pink (approximately 2–4 minutes, depending on size). Stir in lemon juice and parsley.

3. Add pasta to sauce, mix together, and serve.

photo courtesy of Dan Zigler Photography

SPAGHETTI AGLIO E OLIO Serves 4

I think of this as an after the discotheque (nightclub) dish to have with friends. It is beloved by many Italians and is my all-time favorite pasta. It reminds me of my long-lost teenage years when I prepared this simple but flavorful dish after 2:00 a.m. with friends.

2 tablespoons kosher salt

1 pound dry linguine pasta

⅓ cup olive oil

8 large garlic cloves, sliced

½ teaspoon crushed red pepper flakes

1 cup grated Parmesan cheese

1. Bring water and kosher salt to boil in a large pot (approximately 1 gallon). Cook pasta in water until tender and set aside.

2. Heat olive oil over medium heat in a large skillet. Add garlic and cook until golden brown (approximately 2 minutes). Be careful not to burn the garlic. Add red pepper flakes and cook for 30 seconds longer.

3. Add drained pasta to skillet. Turn off heat and toss. Add Parmesan cheese. Allow to rest for 5 minutes to absorb sauce. Plate and serve warm.

photo courtesy of Dan Zigler Photography

VEAL OSSO BUCO Serves 4

Veal is a piece of meat frequently used in Italian cooking and a must on my menu. Osso buco is a special dish to serve for dinner because the slow-cooked meat is always tender and practically melts in your mouth. I serve mine over a bed of gnocchi, incorporating the braising juices from the veal.

2 tablespoons olive oil

4 (12-ounce) veal shanks

½ gallon veal or beef stock

1 onion, chopped

4 carrots, chopped

5 stalks of celery, chopped

4 bay leaves

Salt and pepper to taste

24 ounces gnocchi

1. Preheat oven to 300° F.

2. In large sauté pan, heat olive oil and sear both sides of the veal shanks. Place shanks in a large ovenproof pot, and fill with stock until veal is completely covered.

3. Sauté onion, carrots, and celery until lightly browned, and then add to the pot with veal and stock. Add bay leaves, salt, and pepper, and bake for 3½ hours.

4. When the veal is almost done cooking, start the gnocchi. In a large pot, bring 2 quarts of salted water to a boil. Add gnocchi and cook until tender, about 3 minutes. Gnocchi will be ready when they rise to the top.

5. Drain cooked gnocchi and toss in braising juices of veal shanks in separate pan.

6. Place gnocchi on a large plate (or bowl) and place veal shanks over gnocchi.

photo by Lyle Okihara

220

WHITEFISH FLORENTINE Serves 4

Florentine sauce comes from the city of Florence, Italy, also known as the "city of art." I decided to add the sauce to my menu and pair it with whitefish, which turned out to be excellent when topped with spinach.

4 cups steamed spinach

1 cup heavy cream

¼ cup grated Parmesan cheese

2 tablespoons roux
 (2 tablespoons unsalted butter
 + 2 tablespoons flour) OR
 2 tablespoons gluten-free
 corn starch and water (optional)

Salt and pepper to taste

2 pounds whitefish fillets, cleaned

1 tablespoon olive oil

1. Preheat oven to 350° F.

2. Place spinach and heavy cream in a sauté pan and cook for approximately 3 minutes. Add Parmesan cheese. Thicken to a creamed spinach consistency using roux if necessary. Add salt and pepper to taste.

3. Wash and cut fish into 8-ounce fillets. Heat olive oil in a medium sauté pan over high heat. Season the whitefish with salt and pepper then sear on both sides in the pan. Place in the oven for 8–10 minutes.

4. Place creamed spinach over whitefish fillets in pan then place in oven again for additional 10 minutes or until cooked throughout.

5. Remove from oven and serve.

photo by Navid Zadeh

223

DESSERTS

APPLE TART   Serves 2 (makes two 5-inch tarts)

Tarte aux pomme was a daily homemade dessert in my home courtesy of Mamma Caterina. Because of my special association with it, it will always be on my menu.

1 (8-ounce) sheet frozen puff pastry

4 ounces almond paste (marzipan)

1 large Washington red apple

1 tablespoon granulated sugar

Ice cream (optional)

1. Preheat oven to 350° F.

2. Line a baking sheet with parchment paper. Cut the sheet of puff pastry in half to form two squares. Trim the edges of the squares into circles to form the bases for the tarts. Place puff pastry circles on baking sheet.

3. Spread each circle with 2 ounces (4 tablespoons) of almond paste to within a half-inch of the edge.

4. Peel and core the apple, cut in half, and then into ⅛-inch slices. Layer apple slices in a circular pattern on top of the almond paste. Sprinkle the apples with sugar.

5. Bake tarts in preheated oven for 8–10 minutes, until edges are puffed and brown.

6. Serve topped with a scoop of vanilla bean ice cream.

photo by Lyle Okihara

227

CHOCOLATE ILLUSION HAZELNUT MOUSSE

Serves 10

Illusion can be part of a dream. Adding the chocolate ganache on top of the mousse makes the dessert even richer. It pairs well with citrus segments and berries.

10 ounces semisweet dark chocolate

3 ounces chocolate hazelnut milk

1 tablespoon vegetable oil

Pinch of salt

3 cups manufacturing cream, divided in two

1 teaspoon vanilla extract

1 tablespoon butter

9 ounces dark chocolate

1. Put the semisweet dark chocolate and the chocolate hazelnut milk in a metal bowl and set on top of a pan of boiling water in a "bain-marie," or double boiler, to melt.

2. As the chocolate melts, add oil and salt.

3. Once melted, remove chocolate from bain-marie and set aside.

4. Whip half of the cream to medium peaks and fold in the chocolate base gently.

5. Pipe into desired mold or glass.

6. For the chocolate ganache topping, place the remaining cream in a small pot and boil. Add the vanilla extract and butter.

7. Place the dark chocolate in a metal bowl and combine with the hot cream.

8. Chill for 5–10 minutes and spoon on top of the mousse.

photo by Lyle Okihara

228

CRÈME BRÛLÉE Serves 4

I have always loved the scent of vanilla, and the most perfect vehicle for it is a traditional crème brûlée. This dessert is popular in France, where I spent part of my childhood. The vanilla bean gives it a rich flavor. Just be careful when you use the torch!

11 ounces whole milk

3 cups heavy whipping cream

¾ cup + 2 tablespoons granulated sugar

1 vanilla bean, halved and scraped

8 egg yolks

½ cup superfine sugar, for caramelizing

1. Preheat the oven to 275° F.

2. In a saucepan combine the milk, cream, sugar, and vanilla bean. Bring the mixture to a boil over medium heat.

3. Add the egg yolks to the mixture and whisk to combine. When the mixture is smooth, remove the pot from the heat and strain the custard through a fine sieve. Skim off any foam from the top of the custard.

4. Divide the custard into four 4-ounce ramekins. Place the ramekins in a pan of water and bake for 30 minutes or until custard is set. Cool the custards, and then refrigerate until completely chilled.

5. To serve, sprinkle the chilled custards with the superfine sugar, and caramelize with a propane torch until golden.

photo by Lyle Okihara

DOLCE ZABAGLIONE   Serves 6

Zabaglione is what mom gave to us to make us feel better when we were sick. She was taught that eating eggs with sugar and a little Marsala would always cure the flu.

ZABAGLIONE:

3 egg yolks

4 tablespoons sugar

1¼ cups Marsala wine

¼ cup + 2 tablespoons heavy cream

6 ounces mascarpone cheese

1 gelatin sheet

WHITE CAKE:

5 whole eggs

3 egg yolks

¼ cup granulated sugar

1 teaspoon vanilla extract

½ cup all-purpose flour

2 cups fresh strawberries, sliced and cleaned

Cocoa for dusting

1. Start by making the zabaglione. Whisk egg yolks, sugar, and wine over a bain-marie until thickened and creamy, and then let it cool.

2. Whip cream and mascarpone together in a separate bowl.

3. Add gelatin sheet to egg mixture.

4. Mix egg mixture and cream mixture together and set aside.

5. Preheat oven to 350° F.

6. To make the cake, whip whole eggs and egg yolks for approximately 5 minutes. Add sugar and vanilla.

7. Fold in flour and bake in 9″ × 13″ pan for approximately 15–20 minutes or until lightly golden. Allow cake to cool.

8. Cut cake into 12 squares (or use cookie cutter for different shapes).

9. Place a single cake layer on 6 separate plates and then top with a layer of sliced strawberries and a layer of zabaglione cream. Top with another cake layer, and then cover with zabaglione cream. Dust with cocoa and serve.

photo by Thierry / Premium Paris

TARTINA DI FRUTTA (FRUIT TARTLETS) Serves 4

Fruit is part of a daily healthy lifestyle. It's a must on our menu. Coating the tart shells with chocolate makes these tartlets extra special, and the apricot glaze gives it a unique flavor.

16 ounces dark chocolate

4 (4-inch) baked tart shells

1 cup heavy whipping cream

¼ cup + 2 tablespoons powdered sugar

1 teaspoon pure vanilla extract

1 cup apricot glaze
(syrup made from heated apricot preserves poured through a fine mesh strainer)

1 cup raspberries

1 cup blackberries

1 mango, sliced

1 kiwi, sliced

4 strawberries, sliced

1. Melt the dark chocolate in the top of a double boiler, stirring occasionally. Once melted, brush the melted chocolate onto the inside and edges of each tart shell. Refrigerate the tart shells for 10 minutes to allow the chocolate to set.

2. Using an electric mixer, whip the cream, sugar, and vanilla extract until stiff peaks form.

3. Place the apricot glaze in a small saucepan over low heat, and heat the glaze until it is warm and runny.

4. Fill each tart shell with the whipped cream. Arrange the assorted fruit on top of the cream. Using a pastry brush, brush the fruit with the warm apricot glaze and serve.

photo by Lyle Okihara

TIRAMISU Serves 4

Tiramisu is the number one dessert in my country. It's on every restaurant menu in Italy. Every family makes them in their own style, and this is mine.

3 eggs, whites and yolks separated*
¾ cup + 2 tablespoons granulated
  sugar
16 ounces mascarpone cheese
½ cup orange liqueur
1 ounce Kahlúa
¾ cup brewed espresso
4 biscotti cookies
Cocoa powder, for dusting

1. Using an electric mixer, whip the egg yolks and sugar in a large mixing bowl until smooth. Continue to whip the yolks, gradually adding the mascarpone cheese, until the mixture is thick and creamy.

2. In a separate bowl, using an electric mixer, whip the egg whites until stiff peaks form. Fold the beaten egg whites into the yolks using a rubber spatula. Gently fold in the orange liqueur.

3. In a separate mixing bowl combine the Kahlúa and espresso. Soak the biscotti in the espresso and Kahlúa mixture, and then place the biscotti in the bottom of 4 separate serving dishes.

4. Top the soaked biscotti with the cream mixture and dust the top of the tiramisu with cocoa powder. Chill thoroughly before serving.

*This recipe is made with raw eggs. Please be aware that consuming uncooked eggs can increase your risk of food-borne illnesses.

photo by Lyle Okihara

My brothers and sisters on stage with me on my birthday—family still means everything to me (photo by feder.)

www.artclubdisco.com

ACKNOWLEDGMENTS

Many people have been a part of this project and supported me throughout the years. There are so many who will always be in my heart. It is with pleasure and gratitude that I thank some of them here:

I want to thank my sisters, Stella and Flavia, my brothers, Corrado, Silvano, Eddie, and Freddy; my sisters-in-law, Ornella, Fiorenza, Cristina, and Manuela; and my brothers-in-law, Fred and Silvano, who owns Gi.Co. All my family members in Italy, France, Australia, and the United States. My aunts, Ivana, Flora, and Giannina, and my uncle Attilio for having loved their sister with such devotion; my nieces and nephews, including my general manager and nephew, Sylvano Ibay, and his wife Katie Ibay, director of finances.

I have enormous gratitude to the more than two thousand donors who contributed to rebuilding the restaurant. You will be part of my life forever.

I want to thank Daniele Dolina, my consultant and right hand for the enormous project of the reconstruction and redecoration of the Anaheim White House, and thank Manuela Dolino for her part in helping to lay plans for this.

I extend a special thank-you to the remarkable Gaetano La Placa of La Placa Construction who is helping me to rebuild the Anaheim White House along with Brookfield Homes, KTGY Architects, Applesauce project, Tri-Mark/R. W. Smith, BORM International, Architects of Orange, JllP, Inc., TAIT, CRO Engineering group, INC., Greenspan public adjusters.

Special acknowledgments also to Stan and Jennifer Mueller, Jodi Lipper, and Lori Hetherington; Gabriele Manserviti; Jim and Bobbie Stovall; Luciano Ferrone; Fabio Lamborghini; Dr. Daniele Struppa; Carlo Ponti Jr.; Sophia Loren; Franco Pinamonti; Michelle Whiting and Megan B. Seltzer of Michelle

Whiting & Associates; Louis and Tina Laulhere; Alessandro Gonzato; Maria Elena Infantino, Elizabetta Russo; all of my friends at Chapman University; Easton Miller, Tyler Kring, Heikki Veharanta; Greg Reid; Bennett Royce; Leslie Hall, David and Cinzia Prior; Kim Paul; Jordan Steinberg; Frank Groff; Laura Machieraldo; John Fhur; Brady Ford, Bobby and Danielle Ryan; Luca and Lauren Sbisa; Maria and Barry Sultan; Ester Roi; Mario Bassi; Jiri, Satine, and Izabella; Carlo Tesari and Madame Sisi. His Holiness Pope Francis; Bishop Kevin Vann of Orange County, Giorgio Pedrollo, IDRA hydrothermal company. I am also proud to be ambassador of Casa Sebastiano of Trento for Autistic children.

Thank you to all the Caterina Club donors, corporate sponsors, and family foundations that contribute to ending hunger in America.

I am very grateful to Chef Eddie Meza, Sous Chef Lorenzo Onesimo, Director of Development, Kaylee Duff; Office Manager of Caterina's Club, Erika Arambula; Welcome Home program director, Iris Castillo; Feeding the Kids program director and former Program and Operations Director, Christina Molina; Assistant Manager, John Chavez; Sommelier Franco Pafundo; and the entire Anaheim White House Restaurant crew. Photographers Daniel Zigler, Tony Zuppardo, Evelina Pentcheva, Lyle Okihara Terry, Thierry Brouard, Navid Zadeh, Greg Gorman, Maryam Morrison. CBS journalist Steve Hartman. All the television reporters who've filmed and journalists who've written about Caterina's Club.

Thank you to all the Caterina's Club donors and board members, club members, and employees; John Machiaverna, Executive Director of Anaheim Boys and Girls Club; Robert Santana, Chief Executive Officer of Boys and Girls Club of Santa Ana; Don Rodriguez, Chief Executive Officer of Long Beach Boys and Girls Club; Paul Leon of the Illumination Foundation; Mike Baker, director of the Santa Barbara Boys and Girls Club; Tim Shaw and all the foundations and directors of Boys and Girls Clubs around the country and their staffs, which coordinate with Caterina's Club. An extra special thanks to Barilla Pasta family—you've helped me more than you know.

www.artclubdisco.com

Bruno's birthday celebration with all his family, October 7, 2016
at Art Club Madame Sisi, Desenzano del Garda, Italy (photo by feder.)

It is my pleasure to acknowledge all the children who have eaten Caterina's Club pasta as well as Billy, Christina, and Carolina and her family.

Michelle Kube Kelly, Executive Producer and Bill Handel of the Bill Handel Show AM640 KFI Radio and the entire crew: Garry Hoffman, Shannon Farren, John Kobylt and Ken Chiampou Tim Conway, Jr., Sheron Bellio, Neil Saavedra. Agent Bill Gladstone and publisher Kenzi Sugihara for believing in me. Lara Asher. And finally, I want to give my special friends Robert E. Ramsey and Carol Zarate-Ramsey, without whom this book would not have been possible.

This book is dedicated to my father, Delio Serato; and the one and only MAMMA CATERINA.

Information from the following organizations and websites has been useful in the drafting of this book:

The City of Anaheim

Children and Families Commission of Orange County

International Pasta Organization (www.pastaforall.info)

www.worldpastaday2015.org

RECIPE INDEX

APPETIZERS & SMALL PLATES

Ahi Tartare 151

Duck Legs in Potato Nests 152

Escargot Ravioli 155

Heirloom Tomato Salad (Caprese Salad) 156

Lobster Ravioli with Citrus Sauce 159

Portobello Mushroom Ravioli 160

Scallops with Beet Mashed Potatoes 163

Smoked Salmon 165

Stuffed Calamari 166

Tortellini Caterina 169

ENTREES

Braised Short Ribs 173

Braised Rabbit 174

Cheese Ravioli with Porcini Mushroom Sauce 177

Filet Mignon with Gorgonzola Cheese 178

Gnocchi with Gorgonzola Cheese Sauce 181

Italian Branzino 182

Kale Ravioli in Mango Sauce 184

Linguine with Chive Pesto 187

Lobster Cioppino 188

Lobster Tails 191

Mamma's Spaghetti Marinara 192

New York Steak 195

Pappardelle Bolognese 196

Pasta Calabrese 199

Penne alla Vodka 200

Penne Amatriciana 202

Poached Salmon au Chocolat 205

Prawns and Scallops 206

Rack of Lamb 209

Rigatoni Carbonara 210

Sand Dabs 213

Seared Ahi with Tropical Relish 214

Shrimp Scampi 216

Spaghetti Aglio e Olio 219

Veal Osso Buco 220

Whitefish Florentine 223

DESSERTS

Apple Tart 227

Chocolat Illusion Hazelnut Mousse 228

Crème Brûlée 231

Dolce Zabaglione 232

Tartini di Frutta (Fruit Tartlets) 235

Tiramisu 236

INDEX

A

Academia Barilla, sponsorship, 107
Advisory board, setup, 90
Amarone (wine region), 100
American Dream, 17
American Widow Project, 61
Anaheim community, 35–36
Anaheim Ducks, 82
Anaheim School District Mentorship
    Program, 86
Anaheim White House Restaurant,
    xvi, 27–28
    children's party, 117–118
    construction costs, 50
    customer loyalty, 38
    kitchen, need, 128–129
    menu, change, 28
    psychic, impact, 28–29
    publicity, 34
    purchase, 31
    rebuilding, cost, 144
    service, 34
    wing, addition (grand opening), 49–50
Anaheim White House Restaurant fire,
    123–131
    Barilla, support, 130
    damage, inspection, 131–132
    Disneyland Park, support, 130
    Handel, support, 129
    Loren, support, 137–138
    Marriott Hotel, support, 130
    Ornella/Eddie, support, 138
    Ponti, support, 136
    Stovall, support, 138
    Visit Anaheim, support, 130
Andrea, road accident, 56
Attilio/Raffaella, marriage, xx

B

Baker, Mike, xiv–xv, 48
Barilla
    donations, 75–77
    international competition, 107–108
    Share the Table movement, 79–80
    support, 130
    Young Talent competition, 108
Barilla, Paolo, 108
Bastianich, Lidia, 83
Bison Company, hiring, 143
Bocelli, Andrea, 38, 122
Bonds, Barry, 38
Boys and Girls Club, xvii, xxiv, 6, 36–37, 40,
    59–60, 67, 70, 72, 76, 77, 81, 92
    asset, 68
    Barilla donations, 77
    catering services, donation, 36
    children, excitement, 5–6
    involvement, 37
    pasta offering, xiii–xiv
    reminiscence, 91–92
    service, 70, 139

Western conference, Las Vegas
    speech (2012), 76
Bumi Sehat health clinics, 61
Bush, George W., 38
Bush, Jeb, 38

C

Camaraderie, experience, xxv–xxvi
Canales, Eddie, 61
Cantina Anselmi (winery), 101
Cantina del Castello (winery), 101
Cantina Tessari (winery), 101
Cara Romantica, 140
Carter, Jimmy, 38
Casa Sebastiano, 99
Caterina's Club, xxiv, 43, 52
    Barilla donation, 75–76
    CNN donation, 63
    Crystal Cathedral gift, 141
    donations, collection, 70
    focus, 111
    Hero of the Year finalist, 58–60
    impact, 53
    initiative project (2017), 73
    Italian businesses/organizations
        assistance, 99
    KFI radiothon, 69–70
    location, change, 129
    menu, planning, xxv
    model, usage, 88
    potential, achievement, 64–65
    presentation, 103
    reminiscences, 92–95
    speaking, enjoyment, 100
    Thanksgiving dinner (2007), xxvi
Caterino, Delio (meeting), xviii–xx
Catholicism, knowledge, 11–12

Chaillevois
Chiao, Leroy, 38
Chao, Fifi, 78
Charity
    creation, dedication/work, 90
    501(c)(3) status, 89
    legal requirements, 89–90
    promotion, 89
Chef Bruno Hospitality Academy, 85, 86
    focus, 111
Chef Bruno Hospitality Program
    Crystal Cathedral gift, 141
    plans, 140
Children
    diet, 77
    growth/maturation, 86
    learning, ability, 67–68
    "motel kids," xvii, 40–45
    pasta, cooking, 14
    physical activity, 81
    problems, 78
    starvation, xv–xvi
    USDA meal programs, 72
Christ Cathedral, 140–141
Christening, 8
Christina
    hard times, 41–42
    selflessness, 43
Ciba California, 77
Clerici, Antonella, 87
CNN Heroes Award, 61–64
Coffele (winery), 101
Coletti, Giovanni
Communities
    focal point, 86
    return, 88–90
Cooper, Anderson, 58

Corrado, xxi
    death, 2, 115
Couric, Katie, 51
Craig, Jenny, 38
Credit problems, 42–43
Crystal Cathedral, 141
Curtis, Jamie Lee, 38

D

Dalai Lama, 91, 96
Dal Forno (winery), 101
Davis, Taryn, 61
Delio
    assistance, xviii
    Caterina, meeting, xviii–xx
DeVito, Danny, 38
Dimiceli, Sal, 61
Di Penta, Joe/Jessica, 82
Dishwasher, initial job, 21
Disneyland, xiv, 122
Disneyland Park, support, 130
Disneyland, visit, 36
Dreams, 11
Durum wheat, harvest, 80

E

Economic crisis, 85
Emigration, history, 3–4
Emilia Romagna region, 103
Employees, challenges, 44
English, learning, 18, 20–21
    difficulty, 21–22

F

Family
    importance, 10
    life, 3
    "motel" families, 254
    reuniting, 12–13
    values, experience, xxv–xxvi
    visit (Italy), 8–9
Fascism, impact, xxi–xxii
Fast foods, consumption, 81
Feeding the Kids in America program, xxiv, 39
    focus, 111
Felicetti, Riccardo, 77
Ferrara, Power of Pasta
    campaign, 87–88
    party, 103
Ferrara, support, 106
Ferrone, Luciano, 100
Fessel, Steve, 144
Fettuccine, making, 5
Fiscal sponsor, 501(c)(3) status, 89
501(c)(3) status, application, 89
Flavia, 30, 97
FONDAPS, 62
Fondazione Trentina per l'Autismo, 99
Food
    distribution problem, 72
    drive, conclusion, 104
France
    exit, 12
    life, 4–5, 7
French
    dishes, learning, 14
    speaking, 13
Fuccinari, Clementine, 27

G

Gabor, Eva, 38
Galilei, Galileo, 106
Garbole (winery), 101
Germani, William, 143

Giovanni, Nonna (visit), 9–10

Giovanni Rana Pastificio (restaurant), 111

Global Entrepreneurship Initiative Forum
  (United Nations), 110

Global Soap Project, 61

Glycemic index, 82, 84

God, belief, 11–12

Golden Girls, The, 122

Gorman, Greg, 38, 145

Green Card, arrival, 31

Greenspan (adjuster), 143

Gridiron Heroes, 61

Groff, Frank, 144

Guarda, Maria, xxiv

Guests, specialness, xxv

H

Handel, Bill, 53, 67, 70, 129

Hartman, Steve, 51–52, 139

Heroes, impact, 47

Hero of the Year Award to Bruno (CNN), 47,
  58–65

    recognition, 61–65

Highway 39 (event center), 139, 144

Hill, Napoleon, 64

Homelessness, impact, 67–68

Hospitality Academy. *See* Chef Bruno
  Hospitality Academy

Human rights, 118

I

Ibay, Sylvano, 34–35, 41, 44, 124, 143

    bills, payment, 47

    fire insurance/details, 143

Ibay, Katy 143

Inama (winery), 101

Infinite Family, 62

Italian, learning (absence), 13

Italian-ness, spreading, 104

Italy

    food, relationship, xvii–xviii

    love/generosity, 97

    pasta, consumption, 79

    return, 22–23

Ivana (aunt), 114

J

Jesus, 11, 47

Jeter, Derek, 38

Jiri, phone call, 123, 124

Judd, Naomi, 38

Junk food, avoidance, 84

K

Kayongo, Derreck, 61

Kelly, Michelle Kube, 70

KFI

    interview, 53

    radiothon, 69–70

Kids Off the Block, 61

Krajewski, Konrad, 95

L

Lamborghini, Ferruccio, 104–105

    Caterina's Club Italian Ambassador, 105

Laon, 3

Latiker, Diane, 61

La Vie en Rose, 69

    exit, 27

    first job, 21–22

    job offers, 24

    rehiring, 23

    waiter, promotion, 23

Leigh, Janet, 38

Let's Move campaign (Obama), 81

Lim, Robin, 61

Lincoln, Abraham, 113

Lloyd's of London, insurance coverage, 143

Loren, Sophia, 75, 137–138

Los Angeles Virtuosi Orchestra, 136

Low-emission food, 80

Lumi, Gabriele, 88

Lunardi, Giovanni, 3

M

Machiaverna, John, 128

Madonna, catering, 38, 57

Maître D' of the Year award (1986), 24

Mamma Caterina

    American visit, 31

    care, 13–14

    cooking meals at home, xxii, xxiv, 3, 5

    communication, 65

    death, 115

    engagement, breaking, xx

    expectations, 56–57

    family reunion, 10

    generosity, 3

    guests, specialness, xxv

    love, 116

    prayers, 7

    Raffaella, friendship, xviii

    support, 100

    trattoria operation, 17–18

    truck accident, 2

    visit, xiv

Mantegna, Joe, 54

Manservisi, Gabrielle, 100

Marconi Museum, 140

Marino, Dan, 38

Marriott Hotel, support, 130

Mattia/Arianna, marriage, 97–99, 102–103, 108–109

McMahon, Stephanie, 38

Meza, Eddie, 37

Millet, Patrice, 62

Mission statement, writing, 88–89

"Motel" families, 40–45, 47, 51, 53, 56–57, 67–68, 70–71, 73, 78, 88, 93–94, 254

Mother Teresa, xiii

    devotion, 113

Murray, Kris, 144

Mussolini, Benito (arrest/execution), xx

N

Navratilova, Martina, 38

New World Pasta-Ronzoni, donations, 77

Nutrition, provision (inadequacy), 43

O

Obama, Barack, 76

Obama, Michelle, 81

Orange County residents, struggle, xxiv–xxv

Ornella/Eddie, 25, 56

    support, 138

P

Parkinson's disease, xiv

    progression, 55–56, 65, 116

Parma, UNESCO Creative Cities of Gastronomy designation, 107

Parmigiano Reggiano cheese, home, 107

Pasta

    cooking, advice, 14, 102

    feeding the children, 5–6

    glycemic index, 82, 84

    healthy carbs, 77, 81,102

    low-emission food, 80

sustainability, 80

versatility, 79–80

Pastathon, 67, 70

Pasta World Championship, 107

Pastificio di Martino Gaetano, donations, 77

Pastificio Felicetti, donations, 77

Pastificio Rana, media stop, 101–102

Paul/Miro Sorvino, volunteers, xxvii

Peddlers, visit, 4–5

Pelé, 38

Penne Amatriciana (home recipe), 30

Physical activity, absence, 81

Picardy region (France), parental move, xxi–xxii

Pinamonti, Franco, 99

Poitier, Sidney, 38

Pomodoro, Arnaldo, 111

Ponti, Carlo, 136, 137

Pope Francis

papal audience, 106–107

rosary, fire damage, 132

Pope Francis, recognition, 95–96

Power of Pasta

campaign, 87–88

party, 103

Pringle, Curt, 82

Processed foods, consumption, 81

Public adjuster, hiring, 143

Puck, Wolfgang, 38

R

Raffaella

Attilio, marriage, xx

chaperone, xix

marriage, xviii

Rana, Giovanni, 101–102

Regional dishes, pasta (usages), 81

Relais Villa Bella (San Bonifacio), 109

Restaurants

community focal points, 86

job hunting, 20–21

Richard Nixon Library, 140

Richie, Lionel, 38

Roberts, Doris, 38

Rocca Sveva (winery), 101

Rotary Club, Caterina's Club speech, 106–107

Russian National Orchestra, 136

Ryan, Bobby, 122

S

Saint Anthony of Padua, prayer, 7

San Bonifacio, 13, 55–56, 69

return, 22–23, 108

Sarandon, Susan, 59

Second meal concept, 84

Section 8 families, service, 70

Seinfeld, Jerry, 62, 133

Serato, Alberto, 80

Serato, Corrado, 60, 82, 114, 238–239

Serato, Cristina, 239

Serato, Eddie, 25, 60, 114, 238–239

Serato, Fiorenza, 239

Serato, Flavia 25, 60, 97–98, 114, 238–239

Serato, Freddy 60, 63, 65, 97, 114, 238–239

Serato, Manuela, 249

Serato, Ornella, 25, 56, 138, 239

Serato, Silvano, 25, 60, 114, 238–239

Serato, Stella, xiv, 60, 82, 98, 114, 126, 238–239

birth, 3

marriage, 18–19

SFSP. *See* Summer Food Service Program

Share the Table movement (Barilla), 79–80

Shepard, Alan, 38

Shrine Auditorium, festivities, 59, 61

Simphal farm, xxii

Soave (wine region), 100

Sodas, consumption, 81

Somers, Suzanne, 38

Sorvino, Mira, 29, 54, 118

Sorvino, Paul, 29, 54

Spaghetti, etymology, xxv

Sphere Within Sphere (Pomodoro), 111

Stamos, John, 38

St. Denis, Richard, 62

Stefani, Gwen, 38, 122, 159

Stokes, Amy, 62

Stovall, Bobbie, 138

Stovall, James, 138
    contract, 31
    meeting, 27

Streisand, Barbara, 20

Summer Food Service Program (SFSP), 72–73

T

Tait, Tom, 144

Time Is Now to Help, The, 61

Tomato sauce, classic, 68

Trattoria Cristallo, 13–14, 69

Trento, 99

Triple H, 38

U

Unemployment, problem, 69

United States Department of Agriculture (USDA) meal programs, 72

University of Padua, Caterina's Club speech, 106–107

V

Valentine's Day, restaurant preparations, 121–122

Valpolicella (wine region), 100

Van Asperen (bank supporter), 31

Veneto, xxi

Verona, 1, 17, 114

Vicenza, xvii–xviii

Villanova, xvii–xviii, 3, 9

Virus of good, impact, 103, 106

Visit Anaheim, support, 130

Vivaise, 4, 8

Volunteer Service Award, 76

W

Waiter, promotion, 23

Wayans, Keenen Ivory, 38

Welcome Home project, 43
    baby naming, 93–94
    CBS Evening News coverage, 51–52, 56
    donations, 51–53
    financial source, 70
    focus, 111
    initiation, 44–45
    monetary problems, 47–49

White, Betty, 122

White House Restaurant, 25. *See also* Anaheim White House Restaurant
    name, change, 27–28
    purchase, desire, 26–28

Work opportunities, flow, 4

World Access Project, 62

Y

Young people, unemployment problem, 69

ABOUT THE AUTHOR

photograph © Evelina Pentcheva

CHEF BRUNO SERATO arrived in the United States from his native Italy speaking no English and with only $200 in his pocket. Through hard work and determination, he worked his way up from busboy to owner of the critically acclaimed Anaheim White House restaurant, whose patrons include US presidents, sports stars, and other celebrities

But it's his work with children that has earned him an international reputation. Serato launched the nonprofit Caterina's Club in 2005 after he and his mother, Caterina, visited a local Boys and Girls Club. There, they saw a seven-

253

year-old boy eating a bag of potato chips, and when she learned that the snack was all he had for dinner, she instructed her son to head back to the restaurant and feed the children pasta. Through Caterina's Club, he has done so each day since then, and today he feeds some two thousand children daily. More than one million meals have been served so far and the need keeps growing. His influence has extended far beyond Southern California to include Chicago, New York, Texas, Mexico, and Italy.

Serato has extended his mission by moving these children and their "motel families" into permanent housing. While many of the families are working and able to afford the monthly rent for their own apartments, they do not have the savings to pay the first and last month's rent, plus the security deposit required at the onset of signing a lease. He has already helped hundreds of families escape motel living by finding them apartments of their own and helping with the initial deposit fees through his Welcome Home project, and their lives have improved considerably.

His newest endeavor is working with the Anaheim School District to establish the Chef Bruno Hospitality Academy, which seeks to divert high school students from gangs and other bad influences by teaching them about the food, hospitality, and service industries. In a twelve-week program the students receive hands-on experience and an opportunity to have paid internships in these areas to explore careers in the field following graduation.

For his humanitarian work, Serato has earned international recognition and publicity, including profiles in *People Magazine, CBS Evening News,* and newspapers and magazines around the world. His many honors include being named a CNN Hero, being knighted by the Italian government, receiving a papal blessing from Pope Francis, getting a humanitarian award on the steps of the US Capitol. He has been honored by the Good News Foundation, and has received numerous proclamations, Man of the Year awards, and other forms of recognition—all of which he accepts to generate public awareness of the needs of our most vulnerable population: our children.

For more information, visit www.anaheimwhitehouse.com. To contact us, please email us at info@anaheimwhitehouse.com.

Awards Received

Caterina's Club and I have, over the years, received numerous accolades. The credit, however, goes to Mamma and to the people we've touched. As my way of recognizing and showing my respect for those who have considered us worthy of the awards, and to acknowledge all the people who have been involved, I extend my thanks for their generosity.

2017

Chef Sir Bruno Serato was awarded Culinary Champion of the Year on June 26, 2017, at the annual California Travel Summit (CTS) in Newport Beach.

George Washington Honor Medal—Freedom Foundation at Valley Forge National Awards Program

Humanitarian Award from the American Red Cross/Desert to the Sea Region presented to Chef Sir Bruno Serato at May 3, 2017 Orange County Heroes Luncheon

2016

Excellence in Entrepreneurship—Orange County Business Council

Excellence in Leadership Award—Servite High School

Lifetime Achievement Award—Hispanic Bar Association of Orange County

Daily Point of Light Award honoree—originated out of the White House in 1989 under President George H.W. Bush.

Changing the World Award—Chapman University

2015

"Best Author" in category "excellence in collaborative works"—National Academy of Best-Selling Authors

The Italian Talent Association, award at the Chamber of Deputies, New Hall of the Palace of the Parliamentary Groups, in Rome

Humanitarian award—The Italian Pasta and Sweet Manufactures' Association and International Pasta Organization World Pasta Day & Congress at the Palazzo Italia in Milan

Montale award (Nobel Prize) "Outside of Home 2015"

Francisco Briseno Lifetime Achievement award—Hispanic Lawyers Association

Warriors Medal of Valor—Native American Nations of the United States of America

National Italian talent award for keeping the quality of Italian tradition abroad

❦ 2014 ❦

Speaker of the Year—Orange County Regional Chapter, Community Associations Institute

N-Action Family Network Humanitarian Award presented by the House of Representatives

TV2000, Bruno on Vatican Television

Children's Friend Award Child Help Orange County Chapter

Humanitarian Award Retirement Housing Foundation

❦ 2013 ❦

Pope John XXIII Award—for Outstanding Achievement Towards Humanity, Italian Catholic Federation

Bruno receives the order of "Knighthood/Cavalliere"—on behalf of Italian President, the highest honor for an Italian citizen

Peace Award—Church of Christ in Orange, California

Celebration of Fathers Award—(awarded along with Andrea Bocelli) Simin Hope Foundation

❦ 2012 ❦

Scudo San Martino Medallion—given to individuals as recognition for acts of generosity, altruism and human solidarity (Mother Teresa of Calcutta is a previous recipient of this award).

Americana Man of the Year—Cypress College

Visionary of the Year—Coastline Community College

Outstanding Philanthropist—National Philanthropy Day

Royal Court of the Golden Lion—Sons of Italy